R-3073/1-NA

The Costs of the Soviet Empire

Charles Wolf, Jr., K. C. Yeh, Edmund Brunner, Jr.,
Aaron Gurwitz, Marilee Lawrence

September 1983

Prepared for the
Director of Net Assessment
Office of the Secretary of Defense

APPROVED FOR PUBLIC RELEASE: DISTRIBUTION UNLIMITED

PREFACE

This report was prepared for the Director of Net Assessment in the Office of the Secretary of Defense, under Contract No. MDA903-80-C-0224. It is part of Rand's continuing research program in International Economic Policy, the principal focus of which is on the interface between international economics and national security issues. Estimation and analysis of the costs of the Soviet empire should be of interest to offices in the Department of State, the Department of Defense, the National Security Council, and other agencies concerned with Soviet military and foreign policies in Eastern Europe and the Third World.

SUMMARY

This study develops and applies a comprehensive framework for estimating all of the economic costs incurred by the Soviet Union in acquiring, maintaining, and expanding its empire. We define the "empire" to include the geographically contiguous countries of Eastern Europe and Afghanistan, and the parts of the empire that lie "abroad." The included countries cover a wide range of types and degrees of Soviet influence and control—a characteristic that is not unique to the current Soviet empire. We define the costs of empire to include costs incurred by the Soviet Union to maintain or increase control in countries under Soviet domination, to acquire influence in countries that are candidates for future Soviet control, and to thwart or subvert countries opposed to it.

Previous studies of the costs of the Soviet empire have been concerned with selected parts of the total costs, for example, emphasizing costs associated with particular countries or groups of countries such as those in the Council for Mutual Economic Assistance (CMEA), or with such specific cost categories as Soviet economic and military aid. Our study draws on this prior work, combining and supplementing it in various ways. Even so, substantial gaps and inadequacies remain in the available data. One of our aims is to highlight the most important gaps and thereby provide a basis for further data collection and analysis.

One reason why we are interested in determining the costs of the Soviet empire (CSE) is simply to understand more fully the extent to which Soviet resources are devoted to national security purposes. Direct military spending, for which we already have detailed estimates and reestimates, is of course central to this pattern of resource use. CSE represent another piece of the mosaic, one that both complements and is complemented by Soviet military capabilities.

Another reason is to determine the burden or "drag" on the Soviet economy resulting from CSE, how this burden has changed over time, and what CSE are likely to be in the future. In this connection, we wish to size CSE in relation to the Soviet economy as a whole and to Soviet military spending. With one minor exception, our estimates of CSE are confined to costs that are not included in estimates of Soviet military spending.

Another reason for determining CSE relates to inferences that may be drawn concerning the importance or "value" ascribed by Soviet leadership to the empire and its further expansion. Also, separating the various parts of CSE may suggest ways of raising these costs in the future or encouraging the centrifugal forces that impinge on the empire.

Finally, parts of the Soviet elite structure may not be fully aware of the extent of CSE, as is surely true of the Soviet people more generally. Informing them, as well as informing our allies and such other interested countries as China, of the full extent of CSE may help to raise the level and intensity of discussion of Soviet imperial activities inside as well as outside the Soviet Union.

After brief consideration of costing concepts relevant to the evaluation of CSE, we present a cursory review of the literature on previous empires. The cost patterns and experience of previous empires may have only limited relevance to the course of the Soviet empire, but some historical perspective is useful in considering the Soviet case.

Among the preliminary impressions distilled from this review are the following:

1. Changes in the historical course of empires seem to have been mainly the result of changes in the costs, rather than in the benefits, of imperial activity;
2. The limited available evidence suggests that the normal incremental costs of maintaining previous empires have generally been low relative to the size of the imperial powers' home economies.

The bulk of our study is devoted to estimating the total and component costs of the Soviet empire for the period from 1971 through 1980. The principal components include: implicit trade subsidies; export credits; military aid deliveries (net of hard currency military sales); economic aid deliveries; incremental costs of Soviet military operations directly relating to the empire (specifically, in Afghanistan); and costs of Soviet covert and related activities that can be reasonably imputed to the empire, rather than to maintenance of the Soviet system at home.

Most of these costs are incurred in the CMEA countries (including Cuba and Vietnam) and, to a lesser extent, in Angola, Ethiopia, South Yemen, and Nicaragua, which are within the Soviet orbit, although they are not members of CMEA. Moreover, some costs of empire are incurred in third-world countries that are outside the Soviet empire, however loosely it may be defined. The rationale for including these costs is that these countries may be candidates for future inclusion in the Soviet orbit, or may be targets for Soviet destabilization activities (as in Turkey) to subvert forces antagonistic to expansion of Soviet influence. Such costs may be thought of as "venture capital" costs and "research and development" costs associated with expanding and protecting the imperial enterprise, additional to the operating costs associated with its maintenance.

Except for the *extra* costs of Soviet military forces in Afghanistan since 1980 *above* the normal peacetime costs of these forces, Soviet military spending is excluded from our CSE estimates. This is not to deny that a large part of Soviet military spending might plausibly be attributed to the empire: for example, the costs of naval and mobility forces, and the extra forces (if any) and additional costs associated with the 32 Soviet divisions stationed in Eastern Europe. However, to avoid the arbitrariness that would be involved in attributing all or part of such military costs to the empire, rather than to defense of the Soviet Union itself, and also because these costs are already covered in previous estimates of Soviet military spending, our estimates focus on the nonmilitary costs associated with the empire.

We had intended to include the incremental costs associated with the organization, training, and operations of allied or proxy forces (such as those of Cuba, East Germany, and Vietnam) for which Soviet support has been provided. However, we have not been able to obtain suitable data for estimating this component independently of the six other components referred to above.

Several major methodological and empirical problems arise in estimating CSE and expressing them in current and constant dollars, and rubles. These problems and our efforts to deal with them are described in more detail in the text. To reflect the inevitable uncertainties in the estimates, we frequently present them in terms of intervals rather than point estimates; sometimes these intervals are quite large.

Total CSE in current dollars rose from an amount between $4.9 billion and $7.9 billion in 1971, to an amount between $13.4 billion and $17.7 billion in 1976, and between $32.9 billion and $42.6 billion in 1980. In constant 1981 dollars, the increase is substantially less, rising from between $13.6 billion and $21.8 billion in 1971 to between $20.9 billion and $27.6 billion in 1976, and between $35.9 billion and $46.5 billion in 1980 for an average annual growth rate of 8.7 percent.

As a proportion of Soviet GNP, total CSE varied between 0.9 percent and 1.4 percent in 1971, and between 2.3 percent and 3.0 percent in 1980. The average proportion over the decade was 1.6 percent, with a standard deviation of 0.48 percent.

Compared with Soviet military spending, CSE varied from 7.2 percent and 11.4 percent in 1971 to between 16.6 percent and 21.4 percent in 1980. The average for the decade as a whole was 12.6 percent, with a standard deviation of 3.16 percent. These proportions have tended to increase fairly steadily throughout the decade.

The relative size of CSE compared with Soviet GNP and Soviet military spending changes quite sharply if these data are expressed in rubles rather than dollars. The reason is that the average ratio between the ruble prices for hard curency imports sold on internal Soviet markets and the dollar cost of these imports is considerably higher for each year of the 1971-1980 decade than the official ruble-dollar exchange rate. Consequently, when the hard currency portion of total CSE, which represents nearly 60 percent of total CSE over the decade, is converted to rubles using the average ruble-dollar price ratio for each corresponding year, ruble CSE (which we designate as CSE(R)) rise sharply in relation to ruble GNP and ruble military spending, compared with the corresponding dollar proportions.

In constant 1980 rubles, CSE(R) rose from about 8.6 billion rubles in 1971 to 21.3 billion rubles in 1976, and 42.2 billion rubles in 1980, representing an average annual growth rate of 16.3 percent. As a ratio to Soviet ruble GNP, CSE(R) rose fairly steadily during the decade from a range between 1.6 percent and 1.9 percent in 1971, to a range between 6.1 percent and 7.2 percent in 1980. The average ratio of CSE(R) to Soviet GNP over the decade was 3.5 percent compared with an average of only 1.6 percent when CSE is evaluated in dollar terms. Similarly, the average ratio between CSE(R) and Soviet military spending for the 1971-1980 period is considerably higher than when the corresponding costs are expressed in dollars: CSE(R) as a ratio to Soviet military spending for the decade was nearly 28 percent, compared with 13 percent when CSE are expressed in dollars.

As noted above, the hard currency component of CSE, consisting principally of trade subsidies and military aid deliveries excluding hard currency sales, is a substantial fraction of the total: 66.8 percent in 1979 and 68.1 percent in 1980, and averaging 58 percent over the 1971-80 period. Hard currency CSE are also large relative to total hard-currency Soviet earnings and uses. In 1979 and 1980, hard currency CSE were 64 percent and 85 percent as large as Soviet hard currency earnings and uses from all sources. Hard currency CSE were more than five times as great as Soviet hard currency payments for grain in 1980.

Are CSE relatively large or small? We use four criteria to answer this question: (1) time, (2) economic burden, (3) CSE relative to the comparable costs of the U.S. "empire", and (4) the broad political-military benefits derived from or attributed to the empire.

1. Over time, CSE have increased markedly, growing at a compound annual rate of almost 9 percent over the decade in dollar terms and 16 percent in ruble terms. CSE at the end of the decade were thus large relative to what these costs had been at the start of the decade. They were also a larger share of Soviet GNP, because both the ruble and dollar growth rates for CSE were substantially greater than the corresponding growth rates for Soviet GNP. Whether one views the CSE figures as large or small will also be affected by whether one focuses on rubles or on dollars: the ruble costs of empire are relatively much larger than the dollar costs. In the Soviet context, it is very likely that the ruble figures have the greater importance.

2. To estimate the burden or "drag" imposed by CSE on the Soviet economy, we have used alternative CSE estimates in Rand's optimal control model of the Soviet economy, varying these estimates from an annual level of 1.6 percent of GNP as the baseline case (representing average CSE in dollar terms over the past decade) to alternatives of 3 percent, 4 percent (the approximate average ratio of CSE(R) to GNP over the decade), and 7 percent. Starting from the baseline case, and assuming that the alternative, higher CSE levels were maintained throughout the 1981 to 1990 period, would have the effect of shrinking the possibilities for Soviet growth in civil consumption and in military production. For example, if CSE were maintained at an annual level of 4 percent of Soviet GNP during the 1980s, then sustaining civil consumption growth at a rate of, say, 2 percent would limit the possible rate of growth in annual military production to 5 percent. If, however, CSE were lowered to an annual level of 1.6 percent of GNP throughout the decade, a sustained growth rate of 2 percent in civil consumption would increase potential military production growth to 6.7 percent annually during the decade. For the decade as a whole, cumulative military production would be nearly 30 percent greater with the 6.7 percent annual growth rate than with the 5 percent rate. In general, if aggregate consumption growth were maintained in the range of 2 or 3 percent, each increase of 1 percent in the ratio of CSE to GNP would lower sustainable military production growth by 0.6 to 1 percent per year throughout the 1980's decade. Alternatively, if annual growth in military production were maintained at 4 or 5 percent, each increase of 1 percent in the ratio of CSE to GNP would lower sustainable growth in annual civil consumption by 0.3 percent.

3. CSE are large relative to the imputed costs of the U.S. "empire." Although acknowledging the different meaning of the term "empire" when applied to the exercise of U.S. influence abroad, we construe as the costs of the U.S. empire (CUSE) U.S. economic aid, military aid, and loans by the Export-Import Bank. As a share of U.S. GNP, total CUSE averaged 0.37 percent during the 1971–80 decade, or less than one-third the share in Soviet GNP represented by CSE in dollars, and one-eighth the ruble share of CSE in Soviet GNP.
4. Whether Soviet leaders view CSE as large or small is bound to involve an evaluation of the benefits, especially the political, military, and strategic benefits, believed to be associated with the maintenance and expansion of the empire. These benefits include tangible elements, such as bases and other facilities in Cuba, Vietnam, and elsewhere that increase the effectiveness of Soviet military forces, as well as intangible and unmeasureable, but probably even more important elements such as prestige, political prominence, Russian national pride, and justification for the sacrifices imposed on its populace by the Soviet system. It is a reasonable conjecture that the costs of the Soviet empire, at the levels they have reached in the past decade, are likely to appear to Soviet leadership as fairly modest compared with the substantial benefits they ascribe to the empire.

After considering total costs and their changes over the 1970s, we separately examine each of the cost components. The composition of CSE changed dramatically during the 1970s. Implicit trade subsidies rose sharply from 11 percent of total CSE in 1971 to 56 percent in 1980. Economic aid declined from 11 percent of CSE in 1971 to 2 percent in 1980, and the military aid share, net of hard currency sales, declined from 19 to 12 percent over the corresponding period, although in 1978 and 1979 the military aid share of total CSE was 20 percent and 24 percent, respectively. (Inclusive of hard currency sales, total Soviet military aid deliveries rose substantially during the decade).

Next, we consider without answering the question of whether CSE will be higher or lower in the 1980s than the 1970s. We suggest some of the factors likely to raise these costs and other factors that seem likely to lower them. These factors can be divided between those relating to maintaining and expanding the empire ("production" costs), and those affecting the willingness of the Soviet leadership to incur these costs.

We briefly consider various U.S. policy measures that might raise CSE during the 1980s and thereby discourage further expansion of the empire or contribute to its contraction. Such measures may include denial, or at least restriction, of credit extended to countries within the Soviet empire, perhaps leading thereby to somewhat greater burdens being imposed by members of the empire on the Soviet economy itself. Another measure would be the development of some means of countering the adroit and low-cost use by the Soviet Union of allied or proxy forces, such as those from Cuba and East Germany, in providing the military force to support wars of national liberation. The United States might try to develop a collaborative group of "associated country forces," drawing for the purpose on Third World countries having interests that converge with those of the United States in providing a counter to the Soviet use of its own allied forces. Such a development would require changes in U.S. declaratory policies, as well as in economic and security assistance programs, that we only touch on.

We conclude with a number of suggestions concerning additional data and further analysis that would improve the preliminary estimates presented in this study.

- Estimating the incremental costs associated with Soviet use of allied or proxy forces in third areas, to the extent these costs are not already included in the cost categories of our CSE estimates;
- Estimating the incremental costs, if any, connected with the stationing of 32 Soviet divisions in Eastern Europe, and with the construction and operation of Soviet bases in Cuba, Vietnam, and elsewhere;
- Making proper allowance for economic offsets obtained by the Soviet Union that reduce the net costs of empire (for example, hard currency payments received by Soviet technicians in foreign countries, and the importation of labor from the external empire paid at wages below their marginal productivity);
- Updating the estimates to cover 1981–1983.

Finally, we believe it worthwhile to disseminate more information concerning CSE, both within the the Soviet Union and within the Western alliance. Consideration should also be given to establishing within the government a system for tracking on a regular and current basis changes that take place in the continuing costs of the Soviet empire.

ACKNOWLEDGMENTS

The authors are indebted for numerous valuable comments on an early draft of this report, and for suggestions concerning its revision, to participants in a small conference held in Washington in June 1983 to discuss the draft and its general subject. We particularly benefited from comments by Vladimir Treml, Gregory Grossman, Maurice Ernst, Paul Henze, Samuel Huntington, Martin Shubik, Pat Parker, Harry Rowen, James Roche and Raymond Vernon. Of course, none of them bears any responsibility for whether and how we may have followed their suggestions.

We also wish to acknowledge the detailed and useful comments we received on the earlier draft from our Rand colleagues Alex Alexiev and Arthur Alexander.

CONTENTS

PREFACE iii

SUMMARY vii

ACKNOWLEDGMENTS xiii

FIGURES AND TABLES xvii

SECTION
- I. INTRODUCTION 1
  - Background and Purpose 1
  - Definitions and Terminology 3
- II. COSTING CONCEPTS 6
- III. COSTS OF EMPIRE IN HISTORICAL PERSPECTIVE . . 9
- IV. COSTS OF THE SOVIET EMPIRE 13
  - Total Dollar Costs 15
  - Hard Currency Costs 19
  - Ruble Costs 22
  - Component Costs of the Soviet Empire 27
  - Trade Subsidies 28
- V. ARE THE EMPIRE'S COSTS LARGE OR SMALL? 43
  - Time Trends and Prior Beliefs 43
  - Economic Burden 44
  - The Costs of the Soviet and U.S. Empires 46
  - Benefits 47
- VI. PROSPECTIVE COSTS AND IMPLICATIONS FOR
    U.S. POLICY 51

Appendix: PRELIMINARY ESTIMATES OF COSTS INCURRED BY THE SOVIET UNION FOR COVERT OPERATIONS AND RELATED ACTIVITIES IN THE SOVIET EMPIRE 57

FIGURES

1. Costs of the Soviet Empire in Current and Constant Dollars, 1971–1980 18
2. Dollar Costs of the Soviet Empire (CSE) Compared with GNP and Military Spending, 1971–1980 21
3. Ruble Costs of the Soviet Empire (CSE) Compared with GNP and Military Spending, 1971–1980 27
4. Effects of Alternative Costs of Empire on Growth of Soviet Civil Consumption and Military Production, 1980–1990 45
5. Benefits Derived or "Perceived" from the Soviet Empire 49

TABLES

1. Costs of the Soviet Empire, 1971–1980 16
2. Costs of the Soviet Empire Compared with Soviet GNP and Soviet Military Spending, 1971–1980 20
3. Hard Currency Costs of the Soviet Empire, 1971–1980 23
4. Costs of Soveit Empire, 1971–1980 25
5. CSE Compared with Soviet GNP and Soviet Defense Spending, 1971–1980 26
6. Estimates of Soviet Trade Subsidies 29
7. Soviet Export Surpluses (and Implicit Trade Credits) with Selected Countries, 1971–1980 33
8. Soviet Military Assistance Deliveries, 1971–1980 38
9. Soviet Economic Aid Deliveries, 1971–1980 39
10. Estimates of Incremental Costs of Soviet Military Operations in Afghanistan 40
11. Effects of Alternative Costs of Empire on Growth of Soviet Civil Consumption and Military Production, 1980–1990 45
12. Costs of the Soviet Empire Compared with Costs of U.S. Empire, 1971–1980 48
A.1. Estimated Costs of the Soviet Empire, for Covert and Related Operations, 1980 63
A.2. Comparison of Estimated Costs of Soviet Covert and Related Operations, 1970 and 1980 65

I. INTRODUCTION

BACKGROUND AND PURPOSE

Milovan Djilas recently observed, on the basis of long and intimate experience with communism in the Soviet Union and Yugoslavia:

> Soviet communism ... is a military empire. It was transformed into a military empire in Stalin's time. Internally, such structures usually rot; ... but to avoid internal problems, they may go for expansion ... if it is stopped, the process of rotting will go faster.[1]

If expansion of the Soviet empire helps to avoid, or even to alleviate, internal problems in the Soviet Union, its importance to the Soviet leadership is probably enormous. Consequently, the priority assigned to meeting the economic costs of the empire is also likely to be high. Granted its political importance, how much does the empire actually cost the Soviets? How much have these costs changed over time, and how might they be raised in the future?

The purpose of this study is to develop and apply a comprehensive framework for estimating all of the economic costs incurred by the Soviet Union in acquiring, maintaining, and expanding its empire. Previous studies have been concerned with selected parts of these total costs, for example, focusing on costs associated with particular countries or groups of countries (such as those in the Council for Mutual Economic Assistance—CMEA), or with certain specific categories of costs, such as Soviet economic and military assistance.[2]

Our study draws extensively on these efforts, using them in several ways: combining their data to provide more complete estimates of total costs, often resulting in a range rather than point estimates; adjusting or modifying them to resolve or reconcile apparent inconsistencies in different estimates of the same cost component; and, in some cases, supplementing them with our own preliminary estimates of

---

[1] *The Wall Street Journal*, October 20, 1982.

[2] See, for example, Michael Marrese and Jan Vanous, *Soviet Subsidization of Trade with Eastern Europe: A Soviet Perspective*, Berkeley, Calif., University of California, Institute of International Studies, May 1983. Paul Marer, *The Council for Mutual Economic Assistance: Integration or Domination*, 1982 (mimeographed) University of Indiana, Bloomington; CIA, *Communist Aid Activities in Less-Developed Countries, 1979 and 1954-79*, 1980; Joan P. Zoeter, "USSR: Hard Currency Trade and Payments," in *Soviet Economy in the 1980s: Problems and Prospects*, Joint Economic Committee, Congress of the United States, 1982.

cost components that have been neglected. In this process we will also be concerned with identifying gaps and inadequacies in the available data that may warrant further analysis and future data collection efforts.

Obtaining a clearer and more complete understanding of the economic costs of the Soviet empire (hereafter referred to as CSE), as well as an awareness of what we don't know about them, is of interest for several reasons. One is simply the evident importance of understanding more fully the extent to which resources in the Soviet Union are devoted to national security-related purposes. Direct military spending, for which we already have detailed estimates and reestimates, is of course central to this pattern of resource use. CSE represent another piece of the mosaic, one that both complements and is complemented by Soviet military capabilities. With one minor exception,[3] our estimates of CSE are confined to nonmilitary costs, even though Soviet military spending and Soviet spending for maintenance and expansion of the empire often yield joint products (e.g., Soviet trade subsidies or foreign aid may be part of the purchase price of military bases or base rights in Cuba and Vietnam, and Soviet military capabilities enhance Soviet influence and control in Eastern Europe as well as other parts of the empire).

Another reason relates to ascertaining the burden or "drag" on the Soviet economy resulting from CSE, how this burden has changed over time and, in that light, what the future costs are likely to be. It is also of interest to size CSE in comparison with the costs of the military and civil sectors of the Soviet economy, and to evaluate the effect of prospective CSE on performance of the Soviet economy in the future.

Another set of reasons for interest in CSE deals with inferences that may be drawn from these costs concerning the importance or "value" ascribed by Soviet leadership, or imputed by the Soviet decision process, to the empire and its further expansion. Also, disaggregating the various components of CSE may suggest ways of raising them in the future, so as to impose greater burdens on the Soviet economy, or otherwise suggest measures for reversing the empire's growth. Increases in the costs of empire that result simply from the empire's expansion are not a particularly attractive option.

As previously noted, attempting to build a comprehensive set of estimates of CSE is also of potential value from the standpoint of revealing gaps and inadequacies in data coverage as a guide to data collection and analysis in the future.

---

[3]The exception relates to the incremental costs of Soviet military operations in Afghanistan.

Finally, it is possible that major parts of the top Soviet decisionmaking structure are not themselves fully aware of the true costs of the empire. Simply informing them of the full extent of these costs may be worthwhile.[4]

This exploratory paper will not accomplish all, or even most, of these purposes. Our aim is to make some progress along these lines.

DEFINITIONS AND TERMINOLOGY

Before trying to estimate its costs, we should define the "Soviet Empire". There are three different empires: the empire "at home"—that is, the empire that lies within the geographic boundaries of the Soviet state; the geographically contiguous part of the empire, that is, Eastern Europe, and, more recently Afghanistan; and the empire "abroad". This study is concerned with estimating the costs of the latter two components of the Soviet empire.

The empire "at home" has been the subject of separate studies in the past.[5] This use of the term derives from the fact that the Soviet Union is a multi-national state consisting of 15 distinct national republics and over 60 nationalities, 23 of which have populations greater than a million. The internal empire is not principally the result of the communist state, but rather of the eastward expansion of czarist Russia during the century before the Leninist revolution.

The definition of "empire" used in this study excludes the internal empire. Instead, our concern is with the external parts of the empire, consisting of two parts. The first part comprises the contiguous satellite countries of Eastern Europe: Poland, Hungary, East Germany,[6] Czechoslovakia, Rumania, Bulgaria (all of which are members of CMEA and of the Warsaw Pact), and Afghanistan. The countries of Eastern Europe were, of course, traditional areas of Russian influence under the czars, but the Soviets have considerably expanded extent of control.

The second external part of the empire lies abroad, beyond any previous Russian influence and control. It comprises such diverse types

---

[4]There is some evidence that interest in these costs seems to be emerging within the Soviet Union. See, for example, a discussion of Gosplan's new "Methodology for Determining the Economic Efficiency of Foreign Economic Relations," in H. Stephen Gardner, *Recent Developments in Soviet Foreign Trade Planning: The Gosplan Methodology for Calculating Costs and Benefits of Foreign Trade Transactions,* International Research and Exchanges Board, New York, N.Y., June 1980.

[5]For example, Helene Carrere d'Encausse, *Decline of an Empire: The Soviet Socialist Republics in Revolt,* New York; Harper and Row, 1979.

[6]East Germany is not, strictly speaking, contiguous to the Soviet Union.

and degrees of Soviet influence as those exemplified by Cuba, Vietnam, Angola, South Yemen, Ethiopia, Syria, Nicaragua, Libya, and North Korea. Our definition construes this component of the Soviet Empire as extending to the "rest of the world" both in the sense of current Soviet spheres of influence, as well as potential targets for expansion of the empire to the extent that the Soviets are currently incurring costs in destabilization activities in these areas.[7]

The emphasis in this report is on the second and third meanings of the term "empire." These are the areas where Soviet expansion and control are concentrated, the potential areas of contact and conflict with U.S. policy, and where the additional costs incurred by the Soviet economy have grown most rapidly.

The degree of influence and control exercised by the Soviet Union varies widely within these two external parts of the empire. Our definition includes countries that are satellites of the Soviet Union, allies, spheres of Soviet influence, as well as more or less friendly regimes. Yet this variety is entirely consistent with the characteristics of the Roman, Ottoman, Austro-Hungarian, British, French, Japanese, and other empires of the past. It recalls Hobson's remark concerning the "quibbles" about the modern meaning of the term "imperialism," and the "sliding scale" of political terminology along which "no-man's land or hinterland, passes into some kind of definite protectorate." Hobson's point is no less relevant to the current Soviet empire than it was to the 19th century British empire, which was its intended target.[8]

A similarly elastic terminology is implied in our use of the term "empire" to encompass all the various forms of political sway, influence, and "protectorate" that entail costs imposed on the Soviet economy and are therefore germane to this study. Of course, differences in the degree of Soviet control exercised over various parts of the empire are important to identify for both peacetime competition and potential conflict situations. However, in this study, we are interested in all costs incurred by the Soviet Union whether they are incurred for the parts of the empire that are tightly or loosely controlled: Poland and North Korea, for example, may constitute extreme points on a spectrum that encompasses Eastern Europe, Cuba, and Viet Nam (which are members of CMEA although less subject to control by the Soviet Union than are the other members), and such non-CMEA members as Angola, Ethiopia, South Yemen, Nicaragua, and Syria.

---

[7]See Paul Henze, "Goal: Destabilization, Soviet Agitational Propaganda, Instability and Terrorism in NATO South," August 1981, (unpublished manuscript, obtainable from the author).

[8]See J. A. Hobson, *Imperialism,* New York, Gordon Press 1975, p. 15.

Some costs of empire are incurred in and on countries that are *not* currently within the Soviet empire at all, but instead are targets for expansion of the empire's influence in the future (e.g., India), or for thwarting and disrupting opposition to the empire's future expansion. Soviet support for destabilization activities in Turkey is an example of the latter type of CSE, though it is clearly incurred *outside* the Soviet empire.

In sum, we are concerned with all costs incurred by the Soviet Union to maintain or increase control in countries it already dominates, to acquire influence and perhaps future control in countries seem like promising candidates, and to thwart or subvert countries opposed to it.

II. COSTING CONCEPTS

If a Soviet budget agency or accounting office within the government or the party were assigned the task of determining the real economic costs (the opportunity costs[1]) of the Soviet empire in Eastern Europe and the rest of the world, how should it proceed? As implied in the preceding section, an appropriate definition of the empire's *costs* extends beyond an appropriate definition of the *empire* itself. The geographic definition of the empire, however loose and flexible it may be, is germane only to the operations and maintenance part of CSE. Acquisition costs clearly extend beyond the current geography of the empire.

A suitable cost model should cover the following elements:

1. The total or full costs of those activities that relate exclusively to acquisition, maintenance, and operations of the empire. An example is the trade subsidies provided through Soviet fuel exports to Eastern Europe at prices below those prevailing in world markets, or through Soviet imports of Cuban sugar at prices above those in world markets.
2. The incremental costs of those activities that, while principally connected with the "normal" functioning, protection, and maintenance of the Soviet system at home, incur additional costs due to the empire. We exclude from CSE all of the regular peacetime costs of Soviet military forces, but we include an allowance for the incremental costs of Soviet military operations in Afghanistan. The costs of Soviet forces in Afghanistan properly ascribable to CSE are confined to the incremental costs of these forces and operations *above* their normal costs if the forces were deployed within the Soviet Union. Incremental costing of such activities should thus treat the costs of maintaining the Soviet system as fixed, in the sense that they are determined independently of the empire, whereas the costs assignable to the empire are variable. Where there are joint products and joint costs, it is difficult to draw the line between the costs of empire and the costs of system maintenance. Hence, some degree of arbitrariness is inevitably involved. For example, many of the costs of

---

[1]That is, the forgone benefits that would result from the best alternative use of resources devoted to the empire.

Soviet covert operations and related activities abroad should probably be viewed as primarily connected to maintenance of the Soviet system, rather than to the empire. Other categories of covert operations, such as those involved in equipping and training terrorists in Turkey to destabilize that NATO regime, should probably be considered as elements of CSE, rather than of system maintenance.

3. Some incremental costs that are properly ascribed to CSE take the form of tangible investment or capital projects, provided these are directly related to the external empire rather than to maintaining the internal system. For example, construction of roads to the Afghan border, and improvement of airports and roads within Afghanistan, should properly be considered as CSE, even though they consist of durable investments. Costs that represent investment costs in the standard context of national economic accounting may become variable costs in the CSE context. However, the extra POL and ammunition expenditure incurred in Soviet operations in Afghanistan are incremental costs in both contexts.

In calculating CSE, we include the full costs of the following elements: trade subsidies as defined above, foreign economic and military aid (estimated at their opportunity cost prices, but net of aid repayments and hard currency military sales), and most of the foreign credits (balance of payment surpluses) incurred by the Soviet Union. We include as incremental costs only the extra costs incurred by the Soviet military forces involved in operations in Afghanistan. We should include, but lack the data to do so, the incremental costs to the Soviet military arising from the support it provides to Cuban and East German allied or "proxy" forces operating abroad. We do not include in CSE any other costs of the Soviet military establishment. We thus implicitly assume that the size, as well as equipment, costs of Soviet military forces—naval as well as ground forces—are determined independently of the empire, an assumption justified less by its compelling logic than by the difficulty and arbitrariness of imputing part of military costs to the empire and part to national defense.

We also include as incremental costs a somewhat arbitrarily determined proportion of the costs of Soviet covert operations, comprising activities conducted abroad. This proportion is determined by attributing all of the estimated costs of Soviet KGB and MVD personnel abroad to CSE, but none of the estimated costs of MVD and KGB personnel stationed within the Soviet Union. This is clearly an oversimplification because some of the personnel within the Soviet Union are engaged in activities relating to the empire's maintenance or expansion, and some Soviet agents abroad are also engaged in counterintelligence activities that relate to system maintenance at home.

Suitable allowance should be made for economic offsets to some of these costs. In estimating CSE, our hypothetical Soviet accounting agency should take account of the economic benefits that offset part of these costs, if it were to arrive at an accurate net figure. Examples of such offsets include the following: the asset value of debt owed by the empire to the Soviet Union; labor supplied to the Soviet Union by client states at wages below marginal products; direct payments to the Soviet Union by client states for "services" (e.g., military or technical) rendered to them; and the possible overvaluation of the "transferable ruble" utilized by the Soviet Union in its trade with other CMEA members. A still more elusive offset is entailed in the use of some parts of the empire—e.g., East Germany—as channels for acquiring Western technology.

Although all of these elements should be included in an ideal cost model, our ability to do so in the preliminary estimates that follow is severely limited by the available data.

III. COSTS OF EMPIRE IN HISTORICAL PERSPECTIVE

To provide background for analyzing CSE, we have made a cursory review of the literature on previous empires to see what impressions or insights they might provide concerning the cost patterns of other empires in the past.

One reason for seeking historical perspective is that, without it, we would perhaps be more prone to misinterpret estimates of the magnitude and time pattern of CSE. As with a private firm, a high rate of cash outflow from the coffers of an imperial power might, in differing circumstances, suggest a high rate of investment and future growth, a stable but high rate of activity, or an incipient bankruptcy. Our aim in looking at historical precedents was to identify such cost patterns or other clues that might help us to interpret our estimates of CSE more accurately.

Available data on previous empires do not provide a basis for precise calculations or rigorous analysis of their costs. Also, such cost patterns as may be inferred need not apply to the Soviet Union. Nevertheless, we note some preliminary impressions and hypotheses resulting from this review.[1]

1. There is some evidence that explanations of changes in the historical course of empires are more readily found in changes in the costs, rather than the benefits, of imperial activity. For example, among the numerous reasons given in the literature for Rome's fall, a decrease in the benefits of its imperial control (for example, the value of the surplus grain extracted from the Egyptian peasantry) has not been mentioned. Also, the Japanese and German empires were not abandoned until their associated costs rose to unsupportable levels; a decline in the benefits of these empires does not figure prominently in the explanations. The same might be said of the British and French Empires.
2. Many of the major components of imperial costs are extremely difficult to fathom and impossible to quantify. For example, how is one to value the demoralization of Roman society resulting from long dependence on imperial booty for the

---

[1] A more complete exposition is presented in backup material developed by Aaron Gurwitz for this study.

city's food supply; and how could one estimate the social cost of Britain's century-long export of some of its best potential middle managers to India? Quantitative estimates must therefore be confined to the more readily accessible cost components, even if these amount to only a small proportion of the real societal costs of empires. Furthermore, even these cost components are covered incompletely. Available sources don't provide reliable estimates of the separate cost elements, but rather only partial accounts of total costs at sporadic periods of each empire's development.

3. Nevertheless, the limited available evidence suggests that the total incremental costs of maintaining previous empires have generally been low relative to the size of the imperial power's home economy. Only when direct conflicts have arisen among imperial powers, or when a particular empire has sought to expand into densely populated, fairly well-organized regions, have the costs of empire amounted to a noticeable proportion of metropolitan GNP. For example, the costs of the British Empire became appreciable in comparison with the British home economy only when Britain came into conflict with another imperial power, or when British rule was imposed on an unwilling, organized population. The Boer war illustrated both causes of substantial costs.

4. The Japanese empire may be especially instructive as a precedent for consideration of the Soviet empire. Both countries, during their imperialist periods, were rapidly expansionary, but with fairly weak home economies. In the first half of the 20th century, the Japanese military was principally employed for expansionary purposes, and after 1905 and certainly after 1917, none of Japan's close neighbors presented a serious military threat to the home islands. The bulk of Japanese military expenditures can therefore reasonably be assigned to the costs of empire. From 1917 until the beginning of World War II, Japanese defense expenditures were substantial: They seldom fell below 4 percent of GNP and generally averaged in the vicinity of 7 or 8 percent.

5. It seems reasonable to think of the annual costs of attaining and maintaining an empire as following an oscillating pattern like a somewhat uneven sine-curve. First, costs rise as the imperial power expends resources to expand its external influence and control. Next, once the empire's possession or control is undisputed, the metropolitan power enjoys a quiescent period ("pax romana" or "pax britannica"), during which

imperial maintenance is routine and costs decline. However, during this quiescent period, social, political, and economic changes take place inside and bordering on the empire, as well as within the metropolitan society at home. These changes coalesce into active disturbances that the imperial power seeks to quell, incurring increasing costs in the process. Sometimes the metropolitan power exerts itself to regain control; more often the empire falls, thereby terminating the direct burden of its costs.

6. The history of Rome suggests something like this hypothetical pattern, to the extent that the full burden of empire can be inferred from the size of Roman legions in the field. By the end of the Roman monarchy, before the City began its imperial expansion, the army numbered about 22,800 men. In 216 B.C., the year of the battle of Cannae and the beginning of the great age of Roman imperial expansion under the Republic, the legions numbered some 115,000 men. Over the period of conquest and civil wars, the number of men under arms increased so that, at the beginning of Augustus's reign, the number had reached 270,000. During the ensuing period of pax romana, the legions apparently remained constant at about 126,000. However, under the subsequent reign of Diocletian (284–305 A.D.), while the Roman empire was declining, the number of men under arms increased to 500,000, entailing a financial burden that the imperial government was not able to sustain for as long as would have been necessary to reverse the decline and fall of the empire.

7. In general, the evidence suggests that the hypothesized cost-time curve probably conforms most closely to the Roman and Japanese empires. Both were established following the defeat of another imperial power—Carthage by Rome and Russia by Japan. The experience of other modern empires also suggests that the cost of maintaining an empire probably increases over time. However, even though these costs tend to increase, aggregate costs of building an empire have usually been relatively modest. The major modern empires were, for the most part, built on continents not then occupied by another imperial power, sparsely populated, and technologically below the level of the imperial power, thereby combining to limit the costs of imperial acquisition. Moreover, the cost to the imperial power of building and maintaining an empire typically seems to depend less on internal imperial dynamics or imperial management practices, and more on the degree of

resistance offered to the emerging empire by competitive powers.
8. The fall of empires is frequently associated with large economic costs to the imperial power. This is common to the differing experiences of Rome, Japan, and France in both Indo-China and North Africa. In the case of Japan, the empire's fall is more directly attributable to Japan's defeat in war, but the war itself grew out of Japanese efforts to expand its imperial domain.
9. Apart from such cost discontinuities, it is difficult to discern instances in which marginal changes in the costs of empire have had identifiable effects on imperialist behavior. Part of the reason may have been that through most of the history of modern empires the cost of acquiring and maintaining the empire was small relative to both the national budget and the GNP. Hence, it is not surprising that parliamentary debates about the advisability of imperialism often focused more on the value of the alleged benefits than on the cost burden imposed by the empire. This was true in both the British and Dutch arguments against imperialism. However, the termination of empires usually only followed or accompanied sharply increased costs.
10. The literature on imperialism contains numerous discussions of which social groups benefited from the imperialist enterprise. If the development of an empire is associated with the interests of a particular class, then the effect of costs on imperial behavior will not be direct. Instead, this effect will be mediated by changes in the ability of the benefiting class to distribute the attendant costs in the society as a whole through the metropolitan political process. Thus, it may not have been the cost of the empire per se that led the British to relinquish their colonies. Instead, decolonization may have been the result of a shift in political power in Great Britain from the upper economic and social classes that benefited from imperialist activities to the lower economic and social classes that benefited from the equally or more costly activities of the welfare state.

IV. COSTS OF THE SOVIET EMPIRE

This section presents estimates of the total and the component costs of the Soviet empire. In making these estimates, we include costs incurred by the Soviet Union in the nine CMEA countries (Bulgaria, Czechoslovakia, East Germany, Hungary, Poland, Rumania, Cuba, Mongolia, and Vietnam) as well as in any developing or third world countries that met either of the following criteria: (1) incurred a trade deficit with the Soviet Union in excess of $10 million in any single year between 1970 and 1980; or (2) received Soviet military or economic aid deliveries during this period (net of hard currency mlitary sales and net of economic aid repayments).

Third world countries that meet either of these criteria are not thereby in the Soviet empire, nor within the Soviet orbit, in the same sense as are the CMEA countries. Indeed, even within the CMEA, the degree of Soviet control varies widely between, say, Poland and Bulgaria on the one hand, and Viet Nam and Cuba on the other. Soviet control is attenuated though still substantial, in some of the countries outside CMEA that are included in the defining criteria of CSE—e.g., Angola, Ethiopia, South Yemen, Nicaragua, and Syria. And in some other non-aligned countries that meet these criteria, such as India, it is more appropriate to speak of Soviet *influence* than control. Inclusion within CSE of costs relating to all of these very different categories of countries is based on the following considerations:

1. Empires of the past have typically included areas experiencing vastly different degrees of influence and control by the imperial power at the center. A "sliding scale of political terminology" applies no less to the Soviet empire than to the British empire to which Hobson first applied it.
2. Conceptually, the total costs of an enterprise should include acquisition as well as maintenance costs, venture capital and research and development costs as well as operating costs. In our CSE estimates, we view the Soviet empire as an enterprise with which these several types of costs are associated.
3. In this view, Soviet aid to India and to other nonaligned states is analogous to the costs of venture capital in a standard enterprise, and Soviet support for destabilization activities in Turkey may be likened to the R&D costs of such an enterprise. As with other enterprises, many of these costs will not

result in early or even later accretions to the Soviet empire. Management of the imperial enterprise, as of other enterprises, inevitably entails losses, as well as gains; also, as with other enterprises, the outcome for the empire may sometimes be aleatory rather than assured.

All of the estimates should be viewed as preliminary and tentative, some components more so than others. For example, our estimates of the share and amounts of Soviet covert and related activities that should be imputed to CSE deal with an area that is, to quote Churchill, a "riddle wrapped in a mystery inside an enigma." Our estimates are intended to provide a basis for discussion, critique, and improvement.

Our estimates emphasize non-military costs. No imputation to CSE has been attempted for any part of the Soviet Union's own military forces. For example, we make no allowance in the CSE estimates for the expansion of Soviet airlift, naval, or other projection forces in the past decade. Our estimates include only the incremental costs of Soviet forces in Afghanistan above the normal costs of these forces if they were deployed within the Soviet Union. Although surely some of the investment and O&M costs of regular Soviet projection forces should in principle be imputed to CSE, we have found no reasonable way to make this imputation. Nor have we considered as a part of CSE the extra forces (if any) and extra costs associated with the 32 Soviet divisions in Central and Eastern Europe. Exclusion of Soviet military costs is based on two considerations: Soviet military spending has already been carefully and repeatedly estimated, so we do not need to retrace this ground to add the CSE piece to the mosaic of total Soviet security-related expenditures; and, in any event, the inherent problems of joint costs and joint products would make the assignment of a portion of Soviet military costs to CSE a formidable, as well as arbitrary, exercise.

The estimates, although incomplete, are probably "conservative" in the sense of erring on the low side. One major omission relates to the direct operational costs of allied or "proxy" forces used by the Soviet Union. Economic support for the Cuban, East German, and Vietnamese economies is included in our estimates, as are direct military aid deliveries to these countries. However, we have not found data on the direct operational costs of these countries' military forces that have been employed in operations within the Soviet empire. For example, such costs would include POL, ammunition, military equipment, spares, maintenance and replacement costs, and personnel casualties. We do not know whether any or all of these operational costs are already included in other components of CSE for which we have estimates, nor how much of the excluded costs the Soviet Union bears. This is one important gap in the estimates.

Another omission arises from the fact that data on economic offsets to the reported costs of empire are extremely limited. For example, we have not been able to make estimates of the asset value of debt owed to the Soviet Union by the East European countries, Vietnam, North Korea, and other debtors, nor of the net value of labor supplied by some of the client states at wages below their marginal productivity, nor of payments the Soviet Union received from client states in return for Soviet technical or other services. From an accounting standpoint, it is encouraging that this omission has an opposite sign from that of the preceding one relating to the operations of allied or proxy forces. However, there is no reason to expect their magnitudes to be equal.

Several specific technical problems arise in the course of the estimates: for example, in making conversions from rubles to dollars for some of the components, from dollars to rubles for others, and from current to constant prices; and in expressing CSE as a proportion of GNP or in sizing CSE in relation to Soviet military spending. We discuss these problems, and the methods we have used in dealing with them, in connection with the specific estimates.

Finally, to reflect some of the inescapable uncertainties in the estimates, we present them frequently in terms of intervals or ranges rather than point estimates. Sometimes these intervals are large.

TOTAL DOLLAR COSTS

Table 1 presents estimates of the real resource costs of empire, in current as well as in constant dollars, incurred by the Soviet Union in the form of implicit trade subsidies, trade credits, economic aid, military aid, military operations by Soviet forces, and covert and related "destabilization" activities abroad. Details on each of the component estimates summarized in Table 1 are discussed later, and in the footnotes to the table.

Figure 1 shows the pattern of CSE in current and constant dollars throughout the 1970s decade. The vertical band of the curves indicates the range of our estimates for each individual year. The curves showing CSE in current dollars increase fairly steadily throughout the decade. When the inflationary component of these increases has been removed, as in the second set of curves, the increases throughout the decade are reduced, although there is an appreciable increase by the end of the decade over the magnitudes prevailing earlier.

Table 1

COSTS OF THE SOVIET EMPIRE, 1971-1980
(In billions of current dollars)[a]

	1971	1972	1973	1974	1975	1976	1977	1978	1979	1980	1981
1. Trade subsidies[a]	.44-.97	(-)06-.66	.92-1.78	5.69-6.67	5.11-6.23	5.78-6.95	6.31-7.71	6.37-8.39	9.26-13.07	18.47-23.69	
2. Trade credits[b]	1.05	-.30	-.11	.88	.36	1.65	2.78	2.01	4.85	6.09	
3. Economic aid deliveries[c]	.69	.65	.77	.82	.57	.58	.63	.61	.90	.85	
4. Military aid deliveries (excluding hard-currency sales)[d]	1.20	2.30	3.70	2.60	2.50	3.45	3.38	3.44	6.65	4.60	2.49
Hard-currency military sales	(.40)	(.60)	(1.60)	(1.50)	(1.50)	(1.85)	(3.22)	(3.96)	(3.85)	(4.20)	(4.20)
5. Military operations of Soviet forces (Afghanistan)										.50-1.20[e]	.60-1.45[f]
6. Covert operations and related activities[g]	1.53-3.97	1.61-4.16	1.69-4.37	1.78-4.59	1.87-4.82	1.94-5.06	2.04-5.31	2.14-5.58	2.25-5.86	2.36-6.15	
7. Total CSE (1+2+3+4+5+6)	4.91-7.88	4.20-7.47	6.97-10.51	11.77-15.56	10.41-14.48	13.40-17.69	15.14-19.81	14.57-20.03	23.91-31.33	32.87-42.58	
8. Total CSE in billions of constant 1981 dollars[h]	13.56-21.77	11.29-20.08	16.02-24.16	21.32-28.19	16.84-23.43	20.94-27.64	22.83-29.88	20.55-28.25	29.63-38.82	35.88-46.48	
9. Index of U.S. export unit value (1981 = 100)	36.2	37.2	43.5	55.2	61.8	64.0	66.3	70.9	80.7	91.6	100

Table 1—continued

[a] Unless otherwise indicated.

[b] See text pp. 31-35 for explanation of sources and methods used for these estimates. Soviet trade subsidies to Vietnam and Mongolia not estimated due to lack of data.

[c] Includes reported economic aid deliveries to Vietnam, North Korea, and Afghanistan, as well as aid deliveries to non-communist LDCs net of repayments by those countries for the period 1974 to 1980. Our economic aid figures are somewhat smaller than those appearing elsewhere because we have tried to take separate account of trade credits which other references sometimes include within economic aid, and we have also tried to distinguish between gross aid and aid net of repayments. See discussion pp. 31-35, 37. Other references include *Communist Aid Activities in Non-Communist Less Developed Countries, 1979 and 1954-79*, Central Intelligence Agency, 1980; Joan P. Zoeter, "USSR: Hard Currency Trade and Payments," *Soviet Economy in the 1980s: Problems and Prospects*, Part 2, Joint Economic Committee, Congress of the United States, 1982; and other data presented in an unclassified CIA draft paper of May 1981.

[d] Military aid deliveries have been estimated as the difference between total Soviet arms exports and Soviet hard-currency arms sales to the less-developed countries. This difference appears in row 4. Hard-currency arms sales are shown in parentheses below the aid figures. Total Soviet arms exports, based on trade figures reported by individual exporting and importing countries, are presented in *World Military Expenditures and Arms Transfers 1971-80*, Arms Control and Disarmament Agency, 1983, p. 108. Hard-currency arms sales are reported in Joan P. Zoeter, "USSR: Hard Currency Trade and Payments," op. cit.

[e] Based on a survey of public estimates, including particularly the testimony of former DIA director Gen. Eugene Tighe in *Allocation of Resources in the Soviet Union and China--1980*, J-int Economic Committee, Congress of the United States, June 1980, together with an unclassified CIA estimate of $650 million for 1980 based on an unclassified May 1981 draft. See text discussion below, pp. 37-41.

[f] Derived from 1980 costs by assuming operational costs in 1981 were 25 percent higher than in 1980.

[g] Estimates for 1980 are drawn from Appendix, "Preliminary Estimates of Costs Incurred by the Soviet Union for Covert Operations and Related Activities in the Soviet Union," by Edmund Brunner. Brunner estimates that these costs increased 63.4 percent between 1970 and 1980, which is an annual average compound growth rate of 5 percent. This rate was used to estimate costs for the intervening years. Brunner's estimates originally were made in rubles. The upper and lower ends of the ranges shown in row 7 correspond to higher and lower ruble/dollar conversion ratios.

[h] CSE in current dollars (row 7) are converted to constant 1981 dollars using the unit value index of U.S. exports (row 9), from International Monetary Fund, *International Financial Statistics*, May 1983, p. 430, and *International Financial Statistics Yearbook*, 1979, p. 429. This index was used for the following reasons: (a) the real value of CSE to the Soviet economy depends on Soviet imports forgone as a result of these costs; (b) Soviet hard-currency imports are heavily weighted by grain and advanced technology products, which are also heavily weighted in U.S. exports. An alternative deflator, representing changes in unit values of Soviet exports, might also be used to convert the row 7 CSE into constant 1981 dollars. Use of the unit value of imports index of non-OPEC developing countries for this purpose does not appreciably affect the results.

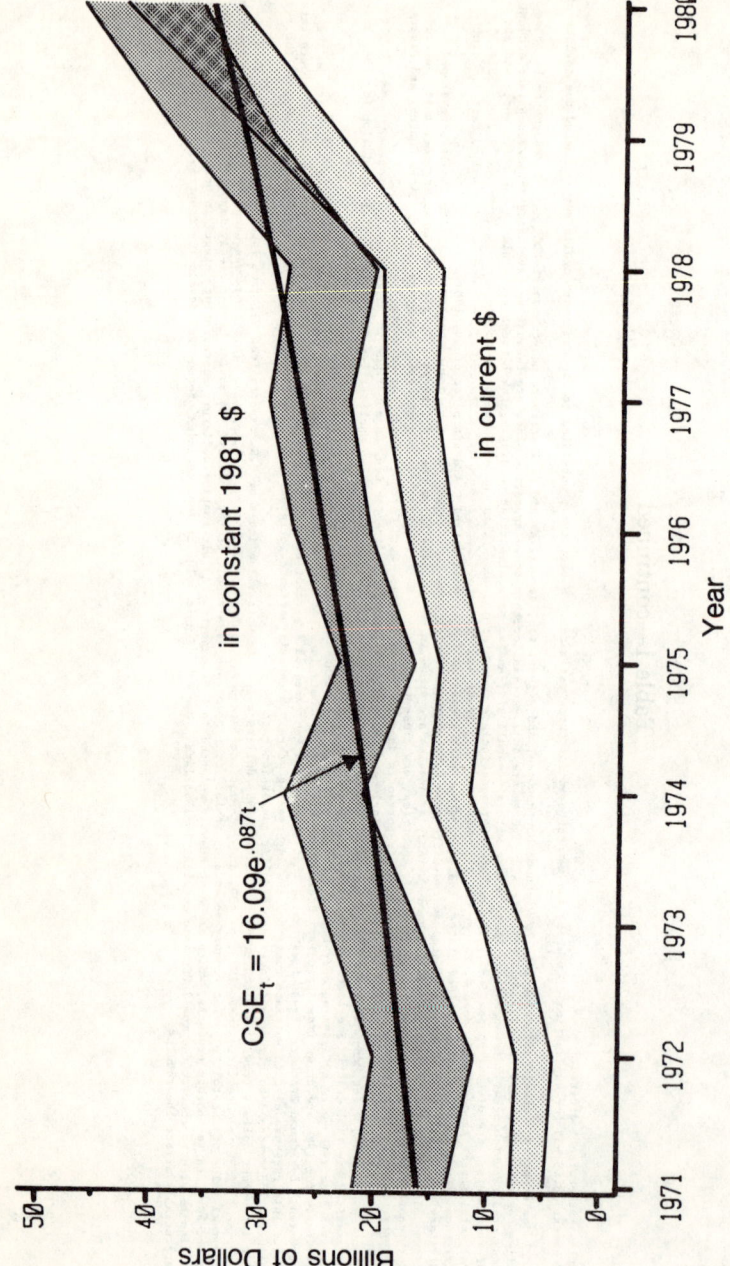

Fig. 1—Costs of the Soviet empire in current and constant dollars, 1971–1980

As indicated in Table 1, total CSE in current dollars rose from an amount between $4.9 billion and $7.9 billion in 1971 to an amount between $32.9 billion and $42.6 billion in 1980. In constant 1981 dollars, the increase is substantially less, rising from between $13.6 billion and $21.8 billion in 1971 to between $35.9 billion and $46.5 billion in 1980, an increase of 164 percent between the lower end of the 1971 and 1980 ranges, and 113 percent between the upper end of these ranges. Average annual CSE over the decade was $24.9 billion in constant 1981 dollars, with a standard deviation of $7.3 billion, and an average annual compound growth rate of 8.7 percent.[1]

Table 2 sizes these dollar figures in relation to Soviet GNP and Soviet military spending. As a proportion of Soviet GNP, total CSE varied between 0.9 percent and 1.4 percent in 1971 to between 2.3 percent and 3.0 percent in 1980. The average proportion over the decade was 1.6 percent, and the standard deviation 0.48 percent.

As a ratio to Soviet military spending, CSE varied between 7.2 percent and 11.4 percent in 1971, and between 16.6 percent and 21.4 percent in 1980. The average for the period as a whole was 12.6 percent, with a standard deviation of 3.2 percent.

Figure 2 shows the variations in CSE compared with Soviet GNP and Soviet military spending throughout the decade.

HARD CURRENCY COSTS

Hard currency resources, whether earned, borrowed, or forgone, are of particular importance to the Soviet Union to finance imports of technology embodied in Western equipment, technology-related services, and grain. Moreover, Soviet needs for hard currency are likely to become more acute in the coming years, if international oil prices continue to be soft and if Soviet oil exports therefore become a less lucrative source of hard currency earnings than they have been in the past.

To estimate the hard currency component of total CSE, we assume that trade subsidies and military aid deliveries (net of military sales) represent hard currency that could have been earned or saved.[2] We make no allowance for the other principal CSE categories (trade credits, economic aid, and Soviet covert and destabilization activities)

---

[1]The logarithmic growth rate, r, is calculated as: $CSE_t = 16.09 e^{.087t}$.

[2]Our method of estimating the total hard currency part of CSE entails some arguable propositions. For example, if world demand for Soviet weapons is less than perfectly elastic, then the hard currency component of Soviet military aid may be overestimated in Table 3. If the weapons had originally been sold to Soviet client states at prices lower than their world market prices, then the estimates of military aid in Table 3 would be on the low side.

Table 2

COSTS OF THE SOVIET EMPIRE COMPARED WITH SOVIET GNP AND SOVIET MILITARY SPENDING, 1971-1980

	1971	1972	1973	1974	1975	1976	1977	1978	1979	1980
1. Total CSE (in billions of current dollars)[a]	4.91-7.88	4.20-7.47	6.97-10.51	11.77-15.56	10.41-14.48	13.40-17.69	15.14-19.81	14.57-20.03	23.91-31.33	32.87-42.58
2. Soviet GNP (billions current US dollars)[b]	573	619	680	770	891	978	1086	1161	1278	1418
3. Soviet military spending as % of Soviet GNP[c]	12	12	11.8	12	12.5	13	12.5	12	13	14
4. CSE as ratio to GNP (1/2) (%)	0.86-1.37	0.68-1.21	1.03-1.55	1.53-2.02	1.17-1.63	1.37-1.81	1.39-1.82	1.25-1.73	1.87-2.45	2.32-3.00
5. CSE as ratio to military spending (4/3) (%)	7.17-11.42	5.67-10.06	8.64-13.05	12.75-16.83	9.35-13.00	10.54-13.91	11.15-14.59	10.46-14.38	14.39-18.86	16.56-21.45

[a] From Table 1.

[b] Soviet GNP in current dollars were developed using the following procedure: (1) completing for the 1971-1980 period the published CIA GNP figures in constant 1981 dollars by interpolating the missing years 1971-1974 and 1976, using the real GNP growth rates for those years reported by the CIA (*Handbook of Economic Statistics*, CIA, September 1982, pp. 38, 42); (2) converting the constant dollar series to current dollars by employing a U.S. GNP price deflator with 1981 as the base year (Joint Economic Committee, *Economic Indicators*, October 1982, p. 2, and *Handbook of Economic Statistics*, 1982, p.39). This procedure involves an obvious flaw because consumption expenditures constitute a larger share of U.S. than Soviet GNP (71 percent, rather than 53 percent), while fixed investment constitutes a much smaller share (12 percent rather than 35 percent). Although we could compute a GNP deflator with Soviet end-use weights, the effect of doing so would be very slight because the separate price deflator for total personal consumption expenditures and for nonresidential fixed investment expenditures in the United States moved at rates similar to one another and to the GNP deflator. Changing the expenditure weights would thus not affect the deflators that we used sufficiently to warrant calculating an adjusted GNP deflator. In the year (1975) for which the deflator adjustment would be largest using Soviet end-use weights, the discrepancy is less than 1.6 percent of the U.S. GNP deflator.

[c] *Annual Report of the Secretary of Defense, Fiscal Year 1983*, II-28.

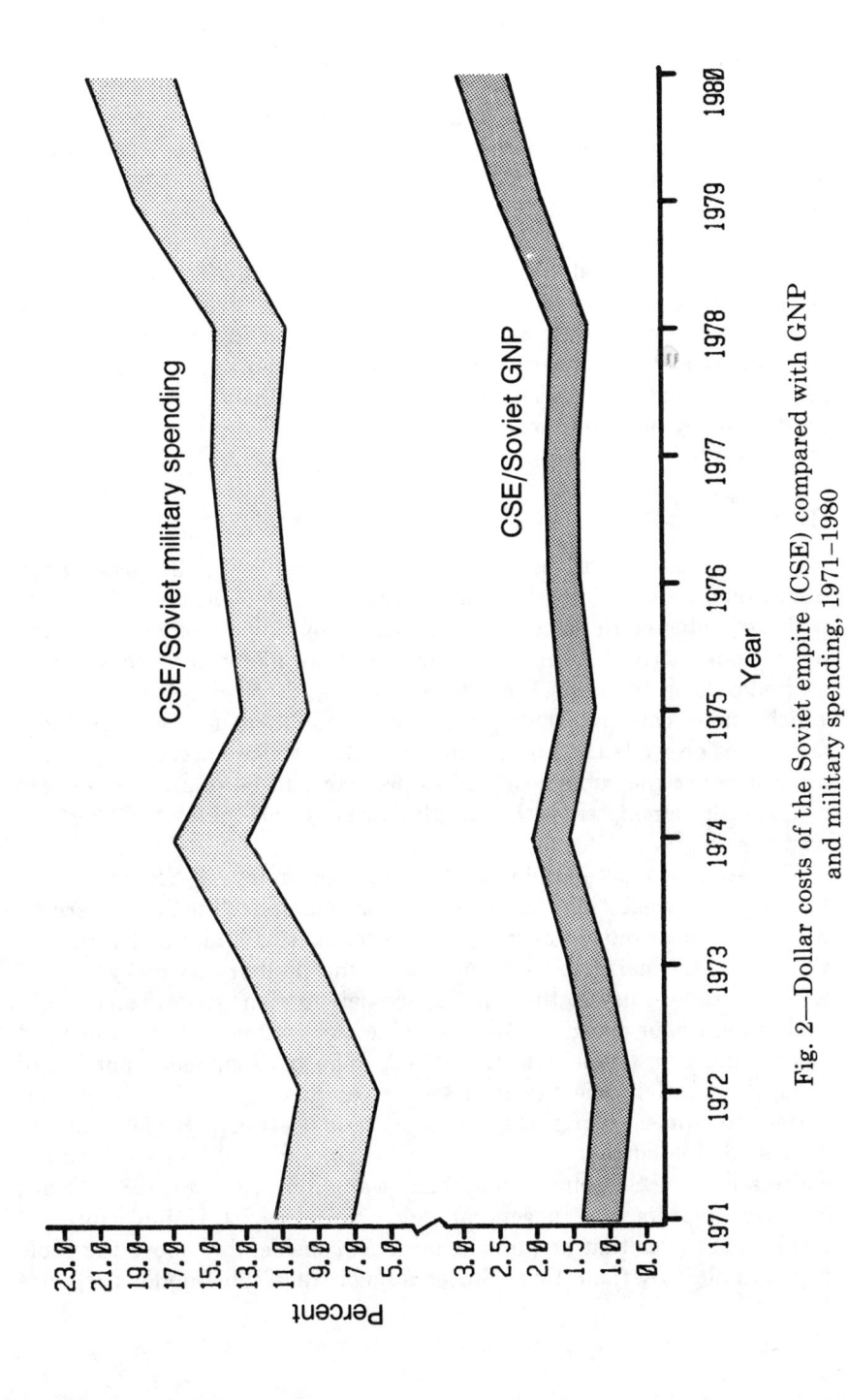

Fig. 2—Dollar costs of the Soviet empire (CSE) compared with GNP and military spending, 1971–1980

in our estimates of the hard currency component of CSE. We have also not included any allowance for a hard currency component in economic aid, mainly because we do not know how much of that aid could have been sold on the world market or at what price.

As Table 3 indicates, the hard currency component was a substantial and rising fraction of total CSE during the 1971–80 decade: 29.7 percent in 1971 rising to 68.1 percent by 1980, with an annual average of 58.2 percent. The hard currency portion of CSE was also very large in comparison with total hard currency supplies and uses to which the Soviet Union had access, as shown in Row 7 of Table 3. In 1979 the hard currency part of CSE was 64.0 percent and in 1980 85.1 percent as large as all Soviet hard currency earnings and uses. In these two years, hard currency CSE were more than five times as large as Soviet hard currency payments for grain imports.

RUBLE COSTS

Thus far in our cost estimation we have dealt with the costs of the Soviet empire in dollars. It is important to supplement the dollar costs with estimates of ruble costs. Evaluations by Soviet leadership of the net benefits derived from the empire are more likely to be sensitive to awareness of ruble costs than dollar costs, and certainly the extent to which wider concern among the Soviet public is felt will be more dependent on ruble than on dollar costs. It is a more arguable question as to whether the ruble cost figures are likely to be of greater concern to Soviet leadership than the strictly hard currency part of the costs of empire.

To estimate CSE in rubles, which we designate as CSE(R), we are indebted to suggestions from Professor Vladimir Treml concerning both the methodology and the importance of this additional aspect of CSE. Our estimates involve converting the nonhard-currency part of CSE to rubles using the official Soviet foreign trade ruble-dollar exchange rate, or using the original ruble cost estimates from which the dollar figures in Table 1 were derived. The hard currency portion of CSE, described in the previous section of this report, has been converted to rubles using the average ratio between Soviet imports expressed in current domestic ruble prices, and Soviet imports expressed in U.S. dollars, for each year from 1971 to 1980. Hard currency imports are, in general, sold in the Soviet Union's internal markets at prices that are, on the average, considerably above the ruble prices implied by the official Soviet foreign trade ruble-dollar exchange

Table 3

HARD CURRENCY COSTS OF THE SOVIET EMPIRE, 1971-1980
(Billions of current dollars)

	1971	1972	1973	1974	1975	1976	1977	1978	1979	1980
1. Total Costs of Soviet Empire	6.39	5.83	8.74	13.63	12.44	15.54	17.47	17.30	27.62	37.72
Hard Currency CSE										
2. Trade Subsidies	0.70	0.30	1.35	6.18	5.67	6.37	7.01	7.38	11.17	21.1
3. Military Aid	1.20	2.30	3.70	2.60	2.50	3.45	3.38	3.44	6.65	4.60
4. Total	1.90	2.60	5.05	8.78	8.17	9.82	10.39	10.82	17.82	25.70
5. As Share of Total CSE (Row 4/Row 1)(%)	29.7	44.6	57.8	64.4	65.7	63.2	59.5	62.5	64.5	68.1
6. Total Soviet Hard Currency Supplies and Uses	4.42	6.33	9.12	11.99	15.51	17.80	17.17	19.99	27.85	30.25
7. Hard Currency Component of CSE as Ratio to Total Hard Currency Supplies/Uses (Row 4/Row 6) (%)	43.0	41.1	55.4	73.2	52.7	55.2	60.5	54.1	64.0	85.1

SOURCE: See Table 1. Figures in Rows 1 and 2 are the arithmetic averages of the corresponding ranges for each year shown in Table 1. The figures in Row 6 for total Soviet hard currency supplies and uses are from Gregory Grossman and Ronald Solberg, *The Soviet Union's Hard Currency Balance of Payments and Creditworthiness in 1985*, The Rand Corporation, R-2956-USDP, April 1983; and Central Intelligence Agency, *Handbook of Economic Statistics*, 1982. The hard currency figures for 1971 and 1972 were estimated by interpolation between the 1970 total ($3.10 billion) and the 1973 figure shown in the CIA *Handbook*. Hard currency supplies include proceeds from oil and other exports to hard currency countries, arms sales, gold sales, and hard-currency borrowing. Hard currency uses include imports of grain and other commodities from the West, debt service, hard currency lending, aid, and errors and omissions.

rate.[3] These internal ruble prices therefore reflect the opportunity costs in rubles of CSE. There is a further question as to whether the higher internal ruble prices more accurately represent real factor opportunity costs or the preferences of Soviet planners.

Table 4 shows the results of this ruble costing of CSE. Total CSE(R) in constant 1980 rubles rose from between 7.9 billion and 9.3 billion in 1971 to between 38.4 billion and 45.9 billion rubles in 1980, an increase of nearly 400 percent between both the lower and upper ends of the 1971 and 1980 ranges, and an average annual compound growth rate of 16.3 percent.[4] Average annual CSE(R) in constant 1980 rubles over the decade were 20.7 billion, with a standard deviation of 9.9 billion rubles.

Table 5 compares these ruble figures with Soviet ruble GNP and military spending. The scale of CSE relative to Soviet GNP and Soviet military spending is considerably higher when both are expressed in rubles rather than dollars, because of the discrepancy between the external dollar exchange rate of the ruble in foreign trade terms, and the internal ruble prices of dollar imports. CSE(R) rose fairly steadily as a ratio to Soviet GNP during the decade, from a range between 1.6 and 1.9 percent in 1971, to between 6.1 and 7.2 percent of GNP in 1980. The average ratio of CSE(R) and Soviet GNP over the decade was 3.5 percent, compared with an average of 1.6 percent when CSE is expressed in dollar terms (see Table 2 above). The standard deviation for the ratio of CSE(R) to GNP over the decade was 1.4 percent.

CSE(R) varied between 13.1 percent and 15.3 percent in 1971, to between 45.4 percent and 54.3 percent as a ratio to Soviet military spending in 1980. The average ratio between CSE(R) and Soviet military spending for the 1971–1980 period was 27.7 percent, compared with only 12.6 percent when CSE is expressed in dollars. The standard deviation for the ruble ratio of CSE(R) to Soviet military spending was 10.5 percent.

The ratios of CSE(R) to Soviet GNP and military spending are displayed in Figure 3.

---

[3] See V. Treml and B. Kostinsky, "Domestic Value of Soviet Foreign Trade: Exports and Imports in the 1972 Input-Output Table," *Foreign Economic Report* #20, U.S. Department of Commerce, Bureau of the Census, Washington, D.C., 1982. As noted, our calculations are based on the average ratio of internal ruble and dollar prices. It has not been possible to calculate the corresponding marginal ratios.

[4] The logarithmic growth rate, r, is calculated as: $CSE(R)_t = 8.82e^{.1629t}$.

Table 4

COSTS OF SOVIET EMPIRE, 1971-1980
(In billions of current rubles)[a]

	1971	1972	1973	1974	1975	1976	1977	1978	1979	1980
1. Trade subsidies	0.94-2.06	0.12-1.29	1.66-3.22	9.53-11.17	7.50-9.14	9.21-11.08	10.02-12.24	9.84-12.95	13.20-18.62	24.90-31.93
2. Trade credits	0.94	-0.25	-0.08	0.66	0.26	1.24	2.05	1.37	3.17	3.95
3. Economic aid deliveries	0.62	0.54	0.74	0.62	0.41	0.44	0.46	0.42	0.59	0.55
4. Military aid deliveries	2.55	4.48	6.69	4.35	3.67	5.50	5.37	5.31	9.48	6.20
5. Military operations in Afghanistan	--	--	--	--	--	--	--	--	--	0.32-0.78
6. Covert operations and related activities	1.61	1.69	1.77	1.86	1.95	2.05	2.15	2.26	2.37	2.50
7. Total CSE	6.66-7.78	6.34-7.75	10.78-12.34	17.02-18.66	13.79-15.43	18.44-20.31	20.05-22.27	19.20-22.31	28.81-34.23	38.42-45.91
8. Total CSE in constant 1980 rubles (in billions)	7.93-9.26	7.43-9.08	12.42-14.22	19.30-21.16	15.39-17.23	20.27-22.32	21.53-23.91	20.13-23.39	29.49-35.04	38.42-45.91
9. GNP deflator (1970=100)	101.6	103.2	104.9	106.6	108.3	110.0	112.6	115.3	118.1	120.9

SOURCE: CSE in dollars from Table 1, converted to rubles, using the official ruble-dollar foreign trade exchange rate for the nonhard-currency components of CSE, and using the average ratio between Soviet imports in current domestic ruble prices and Soviet imports in U.S. dollars for each year from 1971-1980 for the hard curency part of CSE (see V. Treml, "Soviet Dependence on Foreign Trade," NATO-Economics Directorate, Brussels, 1983, p. 6.) The Soviet GNP deflator is derived from CIA, *Soviet GNP in Current Prices 1960-80*, 1983. Since the original estimates of costs associated with covert operations and destabilization activities (Row 6) were in rubles (see Appendix A) we have used these figures in Table 4. Hence, the range of dollar estimates for the corresponding row of Table 1 is avoided because dollar conversions using alternative exchange rates are not necessary.

[a] Unless otherwise indicated

Table 5

CSE COMPARED WITH SOVIET GNP AND SOVIET DEFENSE SPENDING, 1971–1980

(In rubles)

	1971	1972	1973	1974	1975	1976	1977	1978	1979	1980
1. Total CSE (in billions of current rubles)[a]	6.66–7.78	6.34–7.75	10.78–12.34	17.02–18.66	13.79–15.43	18.44–20.31	20.05–22.27	19.20–22.31	28.81–34.23	38.42–45.91
2. GNP (billions of current rubles)[b]	404.6	418.7	456.5	482.0	497.9	529.8	559.6	592.8	612.0	635.2
3. Soviet military spending (billions of current rubles)[c]	50.8	52.6	55.6	59.7	63.9	68.2	70.9	73.8	79.1	84.6
4. CSE as ratio to GNP (Row 1/Row 2) (%)	1.64–1.92	1.51–1.85	2.36–2.70	3.53–3.87	2.77–3.10	3.48–3.83	3.58–3.98	3.24–3.76	4.71–5.59	6.05–7.23
5. CSE as ratio to military spending (Row 1/Row 3) (%)	13.11–15.31	12.05–14.73	19.39–22.19	28.51–31.26	21.58–24.15	27.04–29.78	28.28–31.41	26.02–30.23	36.42–43.27	45.41–54.27

[a] From Table 4.
[b] Derived from Soviet GNP in 1970 rubles converted to current rubles using Soviet GNP deflator based on premise that deflator rose 1.6 percent per annum during 1971–6 and 2.4 percent per annum during 1977–80. See USSR: *Measures of Economic Growth and Development, 1950–80*, Joint Economic Committee, Washington, D.C., 1982, p. 54; and CIA, *Soviet GNP in Current Prices, 1983*, p. 6.
[c] Soviet military spending estimated using same sources and procedures described in note (b) above.

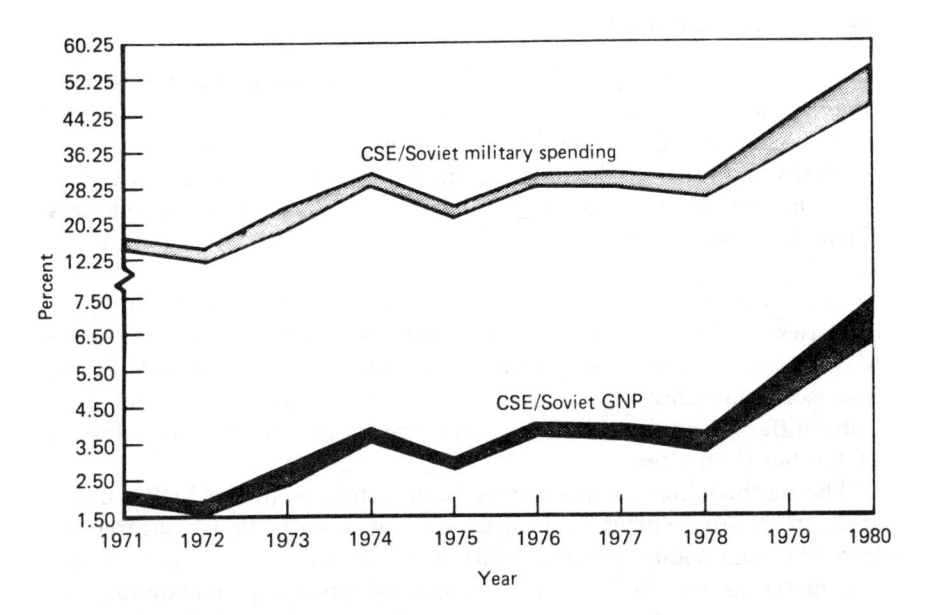

Fig. 3—Ruble costs of the Soviet empire (CSE) compared with GNP and military spending, 1971–1980

COMPONENT COSTS OF THE SOVIET EMPIRE

As Table 1 illustrates, the composition of CSE changed dramatically over the 1970s. The share represented by trade subsidies to total CSE rose sharply from 11.0 percent in 1971 to 55.9 percent in 1980, especially because of the increased margin between world market prices of oil and the prices charged by the Soviets for its oil exports to the CMEA countries. Economic aid fell as a share of CSE from 10.8 percent in 1971 to 2.2 percent in 1980, and the share represented by military aid net of hard currency military sales represented 18.8 percent of CSE in 1971, 24.1 percent in 1979, and 12.2 percent in 1980.[5]

The following discussion summarizes the data and methods we have used in estimating the six component costs of the Soviet empire: trade subsidies, export credits, military aid, economic aid, military operations, and covert and related activities.

---

[5]Total Soviet military deliveries, combining hard-currency military sales with nonhard-currency aid, increased more than five times in this period from $1.6 billion in 1971 to $8.8 billion in current dollars. See Table 1.

TRADE SUBSIDIES

The Soviet Union provides implicit trade subsidies when it exports commodities (especially fuels and raw materials) to its client states at prices below world market prices, and when it imports commodities (typically manufactured products, sugar or other raw materials) from these countries at prices above those prevailing in world markets. Table 6 presents various estimates of Soviet trade subsidies during 1971–1980.

The basic study of Soviet trade subsidies for Eastern European countries is that by Marrese and Vanous (hereafter referred to as M-V).[6] Estimates by Marer and the CIA are based on the M-V figures with some modifications. CIA and British Intelligence estimates for Cuba differ markedly for the period preceding 1975 but are close to each other thereafter.

The methodology for measuring trade subsidies in the M-V study is straightforward. Soviet trade with a client state is first disaggregated into five commodity groups: fuels, nonfood raw materials, food and raw materials for food, machinery and equipment, and manufactured consumer goods. A representative sample of commodities within each group is selected and the ruble prices and world market prices of those commodities are compared to derive dollar/ruble ratios. A weighted average ratio for each commodity group is constructed. Applying this derived dollar/ruble ratio to the trade flows in transferable rubles for a given commodity group permits derivation of a measure of the world market value of the trade flows in dollars. The difference between the estimated world market value in dollars and the actual trade flows converted to dollars at the official (settlement) dollar/ruble exchange rate represents the annual subsidy.

To illustrate, in 1978 the Soviet Union exported 1,242.6 million rubles of fuels to East Germany and imported 18 million rubles of fuels from East Germany. Based on world market prices and Soviet import and export prices of fuels, M-V derived dollar/ruble ratios of 1.77 dollars per ruble for Soviet fuels exports and 1.56 for imports. The settlement exchange rate was 0.86 dollar per ruble. Soviet subsidies to East Germany measured in dollars are derived as follows:

Soviet exports valued at world market prices (1,242.6 × 1.77),

    minus: Soviet exports at official exchange rate (1,242.6 × 0.86),

    plus: Soviet imports at official exchange rate (18 × 0.86),

---

[6]Michael Marrese and Jan Vanous, *Soviet Subsidization of Trade with Eastern Europe: A Soviet Perspective*, University of California, Institute of International Studies, Berkeley, Calif., May 1983.

Table 6

ESTIMATES OF SOVIET TRADE SUBSIDIES
(In billions of current U.S. dollars)

	1971	1972	1973	1974	1975	1976	1977	1978	1979	1980
Eastern Europe										
Marrese & Vanous[a]	0.91	0.66	1.63	6.27	5.33	5.60	5.94	5.75	10.39	21.71
Bulgaria	-0.02	-0.03	0.16	1.08	0.92	0.88	1.02	1.09	--[e]	--
Czechoslovakia	0.16	0.11	0.25	1.17	1.10	1.20	1.23	1.09	--	--
East Germany	0.43	0.33	0.69	2.02	1.66	1.79	1.90	1.91	--	--
Hungary	0.14	0.11	0.23	0.88	0.60	0.67	0.65	0.66	--	--
Poland	0.17	0.13	0.30	1.07	1.03	1.02	1.11	0.90	--	--
Romania	0.04	0.01	--	0.04	0.02	0.05	0.05	0.11	--	--
Marer[b]	0.90	1.13	2.00	6.23	5.03	5.14	5.21	5.64	9.65	20.48
Alternative Rand estimate[c]	0.39	-0.06	0.77	5.28	4.21	4.41	4.53	3.73	6.60	16.48
Cuba[d]	0.06	0	0.15	0.41	0.90	1.36	1.77	2.64	2.67	1.99

Note: Soviet trade subsidies to Vietnam and Mongolia have not been estimated due to lack of data.

[a]1971-78 from Michael Marrese and Jan Vanous, *Soviet Subsidization of Trade with Eastern Europe*, Institute of International Studies, University of California, Berkeley, 1983, p. 43. 1979-80 from *The Wall Street Journal*, January 15, 1982.

[b]Paul Marer, *The Council for Mutual Economic Assistance: Integration or Domination*, 1982, (mimeo.).

[c]Our estimate is based on the same methodology and data used by Marrese and Vanous but employing a different assumption that the East European manufacturers would bring 70 percent (instead of 50 percent as assumed by M-V) of the prices charged to the Soviet Union if sold on the world market.

[d]1971-79: National Foreign Assessment Center, *The Cuban Economy: A Statistical Review*, Central Intelligence Agency, March 1981, p. 39. The 1980 figure is from a forthcoming Rand study of Cuban international debt by Donald Henry.

[e]-- = Negligible or not available.

minus: Soviet imports at world market prices (18 × 1.56),
equals: 1,118.2 million dollars (implicit Soviet trade subsidy to East Germany for fuels in 1978).

Similar calculations are made for other commodity groups. The sum of estimates for the five commodity groups amounts to total Soviet trade subsidies to East Germany in 1978.

Although the methodology is straightforward, actual estimation is beset with statistical and conceptual problems, including the following important ones:

1. Statistical coverage of the estimates in Table 6 is incomplete. Only subsidies to the Eastern European countries, Cuba, and Mongolia have been estimated. Those for Vietnam, North Korea, and other countries are lacking. The reliability of these estimates also varies among different commodity groups because the information available differs for each group. By and large, Soviet exports are relatively more homogeneous products than their imports, and comparable price data in world markets are readily available. By contrast, no samples are available for Soviet imports of machinery, equipment, and industrial consumer goods. For this reason, estimates of export subsidies are more reliable than import subsidies.

2. Lacking comparable world market prices for Soviet imports from Eastern Europe, M-V assume that Eastern Europe would be able to sell the same products at the world market at only 50 percent of the price charged to the Soviet Union. Two problems arise: First, opportunity cost to the Soviet Union should be measured by the world market price of these products if the Soviet Union should import from the West, not by the world market price of Eastern Europe's exports to the West. The two need not be the same. As Marer points out, the price for Eastern Europe's exports to the West might well be lower than the price for Western exports to the Soviet Union, because of Western discrimination against CMEA exports.[7] Accordingly, M-V estimates are on the high side. Second, the 50 percent discount is arbitrary, and may be overstated. Granted that the Soviet Union's imports of manufacturers are inferior in quality to comparable Western products, there are cases where the Eastern European products are more suitable to Soviet designs, because Soviet workers are trained

---
[7]Paul Marer, *The Council for Mutual Economic Assistance: Integration or Domination*, 1982 (mimeo.).

to use them, or because spare parts and servicing are readily available. For this reason, the CIA uses a discount of only 30 percent, which yields a lower estimate of the subsidy than that of M-V.
3. Both the M-V and CIA estimates have another conceptual difficulty. These estimates are based on Soviet imports valued at f.o.b. prices. For the purpose of estimating opportunity costs to the Soviet Union, the use of f.o.b. prices could be misleading. For example, if the Soviet Union were not able to import a particular commodity from Eastern Europe, it would probably have to import a substitute commodity from a geographically remote exporting country. Hence, the ensuing transportation costs, which would be borne by the Soviet Union, would be higher for the alternative supplier. Consequently, using f.o.b., rather than c.i.f. costing of imports may overstate the amount of Soviet import subsidies.[8]

To sum up, the estimates of trade subsidies shown in Table 6 are probably on the low side because of their incomplete coverage. However, there may an upward bias in the estimates of Soviet import subsidies because of underestimation of the free market prices of Soviet imports from Eastern Europe and the neglect of possibly higher transport costs if the Soviet Union were to import the same goods from Western or other sources.

Soviet Trade Credits

Another form of economic cost is a grant or credit extended to another state to cover its current deficit with the Soviet Union, if the credit is extended at interest rates lower than what the Soviet Union could have obtained elsewhere (e.g., the London Inter-Bank Offer Rate). Information to estimate these costs is not available. The CIA

---

[8]The point can be seen by the following algebraic example: Let M and M' represent the cost of Soviet imports of the same type of equipment from Eastern Europe and UK at f.o.b. prices, and let a and a' represent the corresponding ratios of c.i.f. to f.o.b. prices, so that aM and a'M' represent Soviet imports at c.i.f. prices. Comparing imports at f.o.b. prices, one would conclude that there is a Soviet subsidy to Eastern Europe as long as M > M'. However, the correct approach is to compare imports at cif prices because we want to compare the total cost to the Soviet Union at the Soviet border, rather than the cost at the source of supply. There will be a subsidy if $aM > a'M'$, and this is consistent with $M - M'$, as long as $M/M' > a'/a$. Conversely, even if $M > M$—f.o.b. price EE is higher than f.o.b. price UK, there is no subsidy if $M/M' < a'/a$. In general, $a' > a$ because of the proximity of EE to the Soviet Union. Estimates of Soviet import subsidies to Cuba are probably less affected because transport costs to the Soviet Union from alternative sources of supply of sugar and nickel are likely to be similar to those from Cuba.

has used trade deficits of the client states as approximations. The estimates in Table 7 are derived by the same procedure. Because a trade deficit can arise for various reasons and can be financed by many methods, a country's trade deficit with the Soviet Union represents Soviet economic support only under certain assumptions. These assumptions can best be explained by distinguishing the following situations:

1. The trade deficit is covered by either a surplus in the invisibles account, Soviet repayment of a loan, the other country's own gold or foreign exchange reserves, or credit from non-Soviet sources.
2. The trade deficit is covered by a grant from the Soviet Union.
3. The trade deficit is covered by Soviet credit at an interest rate below the current international money market rate.

Obviously, case (1) involves no Soviet subsidy. Here it is assumed that, for the countries specified below, when a trade deficit appears, it is more likely to be case (2) or (3).[9] By and large, the assumption seems realistic. The invisible items in the balance of payments are generally small relative to trade. An extremely large surplus in the invisibles account would be required to offset a proportionally small deficit in trade, and such cases are rare. Most of the states with which the Soviets have trade surpluses are recipients rather than donors of international aid so that loans to the Soviet Union are unlikely. Some of these states may use their hard currency reserves, but generally the Soviet practice is to balance its trade with each trading partner bilaterally.

There are, however, several complications. The first relates to the size of the subsidy. In case (2) the entire deficit is a subsidy. In case (3), the Soviet Union is subsidizing the other state, but the amount of the subsidy is hard to determine. If the loan is paid back in full at a future date, the subsidy consists of only the interest rate differential—the difference between the amount of actual interest payments and the amount that would have been paid at the international money market rate. If the other state is unable to service the debt or repay the loan upon maturity, the loan becomes a grant. In assuming that the trade deficit represents a Soviet trade subsidy, we are assuming that it is an outright or disguised grant.

Furthermore, there may be double-counting if the trade deficit is financed not by short-term credit but by military or economic aid and

---

[9]There are other possibilities. For example, the interest rate may not be lower than the international money market rate. But again we assume that these cases are rare.

Table 7

SOVIET EXPORT SURPLUSES (AND IMPLICIT TRADE CREDITS) WITH SELECTED COUNTRIES, 1971–1980

(In billions of current U.S. dollars)

	1971	1972	1973	1974	1975	1976	1977	1978	1979	1980
Total Soviet Export Surplus	1.33	-.70	.35	2.51	-3.67	-.94	4.30	1.60	6.95	7.99
Communist Countries										
Eastern Europe	-.02	-1.16	-.96	.14	.77	1.17	1.92	.25	1.63	2.81
Cuba	.43	.54	.40	.26	-.50	-.18	-.26	-.24	-.03	.48
Laos	—	—	—	—	—	.01	.03	.02	.04	.06
Mongolia	.10	.15	.22	.22	.32	.44	.58	.66	.64	.72
North Korea	.23	.14	.12	.06	.05	.08	—	-.04	-.03	.01
Vietnam	.13	.08	.14	.20	.15	.22	.20	.22	.46	.46
Yugoslavia	.04	-.01	—	.16	.01	.03	.19	.06	.63	.44
Total	.91	-.26	-.08	1.04	.80	1.77	2.66	.93	3.34	4.98
Middle East – North Africa										
Algeria	-.02	—	.02	.07	-.03	.10	.11	.05	.07	.05
Egypt	.05	.02	.02	-.17	-.26	-.17	-.12	-.07	-.11	-.06
Iran	.04	-.05	—	.05	-.07	-.01	.19	.29	.21	.28
Iraq	.10	.03	-.07	-.12	-.07	-.04	-.05	.39	.80	.33
Kuwait	.02	.02	.01	.01	.01	.01	.03	.05	.01	.02
Lebanon	.02	.01	.01	.02	.01	—	.01	.02	.02	.01
Libya	.01	-.03	-.02	.04	.03	.02	-.08	-.08	-.19	-.19
Morocco	.01	.01	—	.03	.01	.01	.01	.01	.01	-.02
Syria	.03	.01	.03	-.04	.04	.06	-.01	.08	.10	.02
Yemen (Aden)	—	.01	.02	.02	.02	.03	.04	.04	.09	.08
Yemen (Sana)	.01	—	—	.01	.01	.01	.03	.05	.07	.07
Turkey	.04	.09	.07	.02	-.03	-.01	.01	.03	.31	.33
Total	.31	.12	.09	-.05	-.20	—	.19	.86	1.39	.92

Table 7—continued

Sub-Saharan Africa								
Angola	—	—	—	—	-.01	.08	.06	.08
Ethiopia	—	—	—	—	—	.03	.09	.15
Guinea	.03	.05	.05	—	-.01	-.01	.01	-.06
Mali	—	—	—	.02	-.01	-.01	.01	—
Mozambique	—	—	—	.01	-.01	—	.01	.03
Nigeria	-.03	—	-.02	-.06	—	.05	.02	.03
Somali	—	-.01	.01	.02	.02	.02	.03	.09
Sudan	-.03	.01	—	.03	—	.02	.09	—
Tanzania	—	.02	—	—	-.01	-.02	-.02	-.04
Uganda	—	—	—	-.01	—	—	—	-.01
Zambia	—	—	—	.01	—	—	—	-.01
Total	-.03	.07	.04	-.02	-.03	.16	.24	.27
South Asia								
Afghanistan	.01	—	—	.01	.03	.05	.09	-.02
Bangladesh	—	.05	.03	.03	.01	.01	-.01	—
India	-.16	-.22	-.19	-.10	-.14	-.28	-.06	-.03
Sri Lanka	-.01	-.01	-.01	.01	—	—	-.01	-.03
Total	-.16	-.22	-.14	-.06	-.10	-.22	.01	-.08
East Asia								
Indonesia	—	-.01	-.02	-.02	-.03	-.02	-.03	.01
Total	—	-.01	-.02	-.02	-.03	-.02	-.04	.01
Latin America								
Peru	—	—	-.02	—	-.09	.01	—	-.01
Total	—	—	-.02	—	-.09	.01	—	-.01
Total: Selected countries	1.05	-.30	-.11	.88	1.65	2.78	2.01	6.09
Total: Other countries	.27	-.40	.46	1.64	-4.03	-2.59	1.53	-.41	2.10	1.90

SOURCE: Total Soviet trade and trade with East European countries: *Handbook of Economic Statistics, 1979*, National Foreign Assessment Center, 1979, p. 99; same publication, 1981, p. 83. Total for individual countries: Central Intelligence Agency, *Changing Patterns in Soviet-LDC Trade, 1976-77*, National Foreign Assessment Center, 1978; Central Intelligence Agency, *The Cuban Economy: A Statistical Review*, National Foreign Assessment Center, 1981; *Vneshniaia Torgovlia SSSR*, volumes for 1971-80, totals in rubles converted to U.S. dollars at exchange rates given by the International Monetary Fund.

"—" = Negligible or not available.

the latter items appear as separate estimates. In the case of economic aid, such double-counting is possible. In the case of military equipment, it is assumed that arms transfers are included in the unspecified trade totals but not in the Soviet trade data for individual countries on the basis of which the trade deficits are computed. Moreover, as noted earlier, we have excluded hard-currency military sales by the Soviet Union from our military aid estimates. Double-counting of military equipment transfers is therefore less likely.

Just as all trade deficits do not necessarily reflect Soviet economic support, so trade deficits incurred by Soviet trading partners do not necessarily represent costs of empire. The list of which countries and deficits to include is somewhat arbitrary. The working definition used here includes deficits with the nine CMEA countries, as well as with any developing country that either received economic aid exceeding $5 million, or had a trade deficit exceeding $10 million in any one year during 1971–80.

Finally, the estimates of trade deficits are derived from the Soviet Union's trade data, which are valued at f.o.b. prices for both exports and imports. If the client states' imports were valued at c.i.f. prices, their deficits would be larger. To the extent the deficits are financed by Soviet trade credit, the estimates in Table 7 are slightly on the low side.

Military Aid Deliveries

The Soviet Union uses military aid in various ways to support and extend its empire, including the transfer of military technology, supply of military equipment, and training of military personnel. In our estimates of Soviet military aid, we have subtracted estimates of hard currency sales of Soviet military equipment from total Soviet arms exports as reported by the Arms Control and Disarmament Agency for 1971–1980.[10]

Data on military aid are generally reported in terms of amounts agreed upon and amounts delivered. Our estimates concentrated on deliveries because we are primarily concerned with actual resource transfers and the burden they impose on the Soviet economy. If one were concerned with estimating contingent liabilities and time lags between commitment and delivery, the amount of military aid agreed upon would also be of interest.

Information on the financial aspects of military resource transfers is rather scarce. Such information is relevant to the present estimate

---

[10]See Table 1.

because the cost of the transfer depends to a large extent on how the transfer is financed. The transfer could have been affected by any or a combination of a grant from the Soviet Union to a recipient state, cash sales, or credit sales.

In the case of a grant, the cost to the Soviet Union is its opportunity cost—the highest price it could obtain for the equipment in domestic and international markets. Often one's estimate of the equipment's worth in alternative markets can only be an informed guess because such markets are nonexistent or imperfect. At one extreme the opportunity cost could be near zero if the equipment has no international market or no potential domestic use because of obsolescence or overstockage. At the other extreme it may command a very high price, as in the case of air or sea-launched missiles. The point to be remembered is that the statistical measure is at best an approximation and is subject to considerable error.

In the case of cash purchases, the real cost to the Soviet Union is not the opportunity cost of the equipment but the difference between the opportunity cost and the actual sales price. The difference could, of course, be zero or negative, in which case it amounts to no real cost or a profit to the Soviet Union.

In the case of credit sales, one additional element needs to be considered: the interest rate charged by the Soviet Union. Again, there will be a cost if the interest rate charged is less than the international money rate, no cost if the two are equal, or a tax if the interest rate charged exceeds the prevailing international rate.

To sum up, the total resource cost of military equipment deliveries has three components:

1. The total opportunity cost for military aid in the form of grants,
2. The excess of opportunity cost over the price charged for the equipment in the case of sales, and
3. Interest payments due to the excess of the international money market rate over the interest rate charged on credit extended by the Soviet Union for the sale.

In our estimates of total military aid deliveries, we are assuming that there is no grant element or interest rate subsidy in that portion of total Soviet arms exports sold for hard currency. Hence, we have subtracted such sales from Soviet arms exports to arrive at the net military aid deliveries shown in Table 1 above. We assume that this net amount of military transfers was real or disguised grants.

The data shown in Table 8 summarize Soviet military aid deliveries to certain Communist states and to the Third-World regions, drawn from several sources.[11]

Economic Aid Deliveries

Table 9 presents estimates of Soviet economic aid. The data are drawn from different sources and are incomplete. What has been said about the need to distinguish loans and grants in military aid also applies to economic aid. Most recipients of economic aid have been repaying the Soviet Union, suggesting that aid was largely in the form of loans. Because we are concerned with the resource drain from the Soviet Union, only net transfers (recipient country's drawings of Soviet credit, minus repayments of interest and principal) are recorded in Table 9.

The estimates in Table 9 are lower than those that have appeared in other sources because we have taken separate account of trade credits (see Table 7), which other sources sometimes include in economic aid, and also because we have tried to distinguish between gross economic aid and aid net of repayments to the Soviet Union.

Costs of Military Operations

A wide range of figures for the estimated cost of Soviet military operations in Afghanistan can be found in the open literature. Several estimates and sources are shown in Table 10.

We believe that the general estimate given by Eugene Tighe, former director of the Defense Intelligence Agency, in Congressional testimony reasonably covers the annual incremental personnel and operations costs incurred by the Soviets in Afghanistan in 1980. According to Tighe, "The incremental personnel and operations costs amount to only a few tenths of one percent of total Soviet military spending."

The estimate shown in Table 1 was calculated by the following steps: (1) Soviet defense expenditure for 1979 (the last full year prior to Tighe's testimony) was estimated at $166 billion (derived from

---

[11]Research underway by Dr. Moshe Efrat at the London School of Economics suggests that Western estimates of Soviet military aid deliveries to the Third World may be less than one-half the real value of this aid. Efrat contends that the official estimates are based on "major" weapons deliveries (e.g. aircraft, combat vehicles), and ignore or insufficiently allow for small arms, spare parts, communications equipment, and noncombat vehicles. From a case study he has completed of Soviet aid to Egypt and other work that is underway, he contends that *total* Soviet arms deliveries are two or three times as large as reported deliveries. See M. Efrat, *The Economic Dimension of Soviet Military Aid to the Third World—A Case Study: Egypt,* London School of Economics (mimeo.), 1982.

Table 8
SOVIET MILITARY ASSISTANCE DELIVERIES, 1971–1980
(In billions of current U.S. dollars)

	1971	1972	1973	1974	1975	1976	1977	1978	1979	1980
1. Less-Developed Countries[a]	.83	1.22	3.13	2.22	2.04	3.08	4.71	5.40	6.62	4.67
Africa		.06	.08	.24	.60	1.07	1.82	3.09	2.71	
Latin America			.01	.03	.06	.08	.37	.10	.02	
Near East		.97	2.66	1.79	.85	.83	.80	1.89	3.78	
South Asia		.18	.27	.21	.18	.21	.07	.33	.52	
2. Communist States[b]	.43	.70	.46	.71	.25	.36	.31	.55	1.63	1.62
3. Total (1+2)	1.25	1.91	3.59	2.93	2.29	3.44	5.02	5.95	8.25	6.29

[a] Data for 1971–1979 are from *Communist Aid Activities in Non-Communist Less Developed Countries, 1979 and 1954–79*, CIA, 1980. Data for 1980 are from Joan P. Zoeter, "USSR: Hard Currency Trade and Payments," *Soviet Economy in the 1980's: Problems and Prospects*, Part 2, Joint Economic Committee, Congress of the United States, 1982, pp. 503–504. Regional figures do not add to total due to incomplete data from several sources.

[b] Data derived from an unclassified CIA draft paper of May 1981, including Vietnam, Cuba, Mongolia, Afghanistan, and North Korea, but excluding Eastern Europe, resulting in total figures somewhat different from those shown in Table 1.

Table 9

SOVIET ECONOMIC AID DELIVERIES, 1971-1980
(In billions of current U.S. dollars)

	1971	1972	1973	1974	1975	1976	1977	1978	1979	1980
1. Communist States[a]	.27	.23	.27	.34	.29	.34	.31	.35	.63	.57
2. LDCs[b]	.42	.43	.50	.48[c]	.28	.24	.32	.26	.28	.28
3. Total (1+2)	.69	.66	.77	.82	.57	.58	.63	.61	.91	.85

[a] Includes Vietnam, North Korea, and Afghanistan only. Derived from an unclassified CIA draft paper of May 1981.

[b] Economic aid drawings as cited in *Communist Aid Activities in Non-Communist Less Developed Countries, 1979 and 1954-1979*, CIA, 1980.

[c] Economic aid to LDCs net of repayments, based on assumption that repayments to the Soviet Union averaged about $.28 billion a year, as indicated in Joan P. Zoeter, "USSR: Hard Currency Trade and Payments," *Soviet Economy in the 1980's: Problems and Prospects*, Part 2, Joint Economic Committee, Congress of the United States, 1982, p. 489.

Table 10

ESTIMATES OF INCREMENTAL COSTS OF SOVIET MILITARY OPERATIONS IN AFGHANISTAN

Amount	Period Covered
$3 billion[a]	Annual
$2.7 billion[b]	Annual
$5+ billion[c]	Annual
$2.4 billion[d]	1980
$650 million[e]	1980
"a few tenths of 1 percent of Soviet military spending"[f]	1980

SOURCES:

[a] Peter Jennings, *ABC Evening News*, 26 December 1983, citing "American analysts."

[b] Henry Rowen, cited by Richard Halloran, *New York Times*, 23 June 1983, page 5.

[c] Marvin Leibstine, *Washington Times*, 10 August 1982, page 9.

[d] Michael Binyon, *World Press Review*, February 1981.

[e] Unclassified CIA draft, May 1981.

[f] General Eugene F. Tighe, Jr., *Allocation of Resources in the Soviet Union and China--1980*, Joint Economic Committee, Congress of the United States, June 1980, page 26.

Table 2); (2) a range of 0.3% to 0.7% was assumed to cover the range described by Tighe as "a few tenths of one percent;" (3) combining steps (1) and (2), and assuming costs in 1981 were 25% greater than those in 1980, the following estimates, shown in Table 1, were calculated: for 1980: $0.50 − 1.20 billion; for 1981: $0.60 − 1.45 billion. The total cost to the Soviets for the Afghanistan campaign is likely to be higher than these estimates, if the cost of construction and destroyed equipment is fully allowed for. Estimates of these component costs are not available in unclassified sources.

These estimates of the real incremental costs of Soviet operations in Afghanistan are almost certainly seriously incomplete. Specifically, our estimates do not cover the costs incurred by the Soviets for construction of access roads, expanded air runways and landing facilities, and other support installations at Kandahar and other bases in Afghanistan. These costs have been incurred as an adjunct to operations by Soviet military forces and should be attributed to CSE in this cost category. Although the Soviets have made extensive use of local materials and local labor in the construction of such facilities, then use of construction equipment, POL, spares, maintenance, and replacement parts are probably a genuine cost imposition on the Soviet economy itself.

We have been unable to obtain data to estimate the incremental costs borne by the Soviet Union for the operations of its proxy or allied Cuban, East German, and Vietnamese forces in Africa, Ethiopia, South Yemen, and Southeast Asia. Presumably some of these costs (such as the initial equipment inventory with which expeditionary units from these countries have been supplied) are drawn from military aid deliveries and would already be included in that component of CSE. However, other operational costs are probably not included in military aid. For example, the operational costs of POL, ammunition, and vehicles and other equipment lost in the course of combat or other operations may well be supplied from organizations or commands in the Soviet Union that are separate from those responsible for military aid deliveries. In this case, their omission from our estimates tends to bias the totals downward. We hope to be able to rectify this omission in subsequent work.

Covert Operations and Related Activities

Our estimates of these costs are probably the most conjectural of all the estimates presented in this report. The methodology and data, all drawn from open sources, used in making these preliminary estimates are summarized in the appendix by Edmund Brunner. Improvement of Brunner's estimates will require additional work, probably using classified sources to supplement the information available in the open literature.

Brunner's method consists in estimating the numbers of Soviet personnel engaged in intelligence, counterintelligence, subversion, terrorism, and related covert and destabilization activities in foreign countries and applying to these personnel estimates a cost factor, including both overhead and operating outlays associated with their activities. Personnel estimates are obtained from several open sources cited in appendix. We then made estimates of average costs per person, using aggregate data from the figures for total Soviet defense expenditures and Soviet military manpower to arrive at this planning factor. In turn, we compare this planning factor, as a cross-check, with a number of other estimates of average costs per person engaged in various kinds of covert and related activities.

Many Soviet agents and covert activities in foreign countries perform functions that contribute to both the maintenance and expansion of the Soviet empire and also to the maintenance and reinforcement of the Soviet system at home. Consequently, difficult problems arise in trying to impute the proportion of these activities and personnel to the empire abroad rather than the system at home. Brunner's estimates involve certain rules of thumb to resolve this problem. For example, he assumes that all of the KGB agents estimated to be active abroad are involved in activities whose costs can properly be assigned to the empire, but he attributes none of the KGB personnel within the Soviet Union to the costs of empire. In fact, of course, some of the KGB personnel within the Soviet Union are probably concerned with activities relating to the empire and on the other hand, some KGB activities abroad are undoubtedly directly related to maintaining the system at home.

As indicated in the appendix, Brunner's estimates were derived in detail for 1980 in terms of rubles and converted to dollars at three different exchange rates, varying from $0.94 to $2.47 per ruble. Brunner then made rough estimates of the corresponding costs in 1970. Comparing these two time periods, enabled us to average annual compound rate of growth in costs. This rate was then used to interpolate the dollar estimates of CSE presented in Table 1 for the years between 1970 and 1980; Brunner's original ruble estimates have been used for the ruble estimates of CSE(R) shown in Table 4. The relevant cost estimates for the eight different sub-headings involved in covert and related activities are summarized in Appendix Tables A.1 and A.2.

V. ARE THE EMPIRE'S COSTS LARGE OR SMALL?

Whether one judges CSE to be large or small clearly depends on the criterion selected. The following discussion suggests several plausible criteria.

TIME TRENDS AND PRIOR BELIEFS

One criterion for judging the relative size of CSE is time. During the 1970s, the average rate of growth of CSE in constant dollars was 8.7 percent per year, well above the average annual rate of growth in Soviet GNP. In 1971 CSE in constant dollars amounted to between $13.6 and $21.8 billion; in 1980 the corresponding figures had risen to between $32.3 and $46.5 billion. Thus, CSE were large at the end of the decade relative to what they had been at the start of the decade. The growth is even sharper if costs are calculated in rubles rather than dollars. Expressed in constant rubles, these costs, CSE(R), grew from an amount between 7.9 and 9.3 billion rubles in 1971 to between 38.4 billion and 45.9 billion rubles in 1980, an average annual growth rate of 16.3 percent.

Another criterion for judging the relative size of CSE is the beliefs and expectations of the judge. During the 1971-80 decade, dollar CSE amounted to 1.6 percent of Soviet GNP, and in the last two years of the decade to 2.2 percent and 2.7 percent.

When both GNP and CSE are expressed in rubles, the average ratio of CSE(R) to GNP for the decade rises sharply to 3.5 percent; by 1979, the ruble ratio of CSE(R) to GNP was 5.2 percent and by 1980, 6.6 percent.

Whether these shares are judged large or small is thus complicated. It depends on whether the judgment relates to ruble shares or dollar shares, as well as on what the observer expected before these results. CSE(R) looms considerably larger in ruble than in dollar terms. Moreover, the beliefs of different observers outside the Soviet Union, as well as within it, are likely to vary widely as to what "large" or "small" means in this context. For example, Soviet consumers may be more likely to view these shares—especially the ruble shares—as large relative to consumption forgone by the average Soviet citizen, whereas the

Soviet Communist Party and military elite may view these shares as more modest in relation to the benefits they attach to the empire.[1]

ECONOMIC BURDEN

Another way of considering the relative size of CSE is to consider the burden imposed on the Soviet economy by alternative levels of these costs.

To estimate the burden or "drag" that CSE imposes on the Soviet economy, we have used the Rand optimal control model of the Soviet economy to examine the effects of alternative CSE levels on attainable military and civil production growth.[2] Figure 4 shows the effect on potential annual rates of growth in civil consumption and military production that would result from four different annual levels of CSE: a baseline case of 1.6 percent of Soviet GNP reflecting the approximate average level of CSE in dollars during the 1970s; and alternative CSE levels of 3 percent of GNP (reflecting dollar CSE in 1980), 4 percent (reflecting average ruble CSE(R) during the 1970s), and 7 percent (reflecting ruble CSE(R) in 1980), assuming these different CSE levels were maintained throughout each year of the 1980–90 decade. Table 11 shows the results of the model on which Fig. 4 is based.

As Fig. 4 indicates, raising (lowering) the relative size of CSE has the effect of shrinking or (expanding) the civil-military production possibilities open to the Soviet economy by varying amounts. For example, if CSE were maintained at an annual level of 4 percent of Soviet GNP during the 1980–1990 decade, then maintaining civil consumption growth at a rate of, say, 2 percent, would restrict the possible rate of growth in annual military production to about 5 percent. If, however, CSE were reduced to an annual figure of only 1.6 percent of GNP throughout the decade, then a growth rate of 2 percent in civil consumption would allow military production to grow at a rate of 6.7 percent annually. By 1990, annual military production would be 91 percent above its 1980 level if the annual military growth rate were 6.5

---

[1] See the discussion of the empire's putative benefits, below, p. 47.

[2] See Mark M. Hopkins and Michael Kennedy, with the assistance of Marilee Lawrence, *The Tradeoff Between Consumption and Military Expenditures for the Soviet Union During the 1980s*, The Rand Corporation, R-2927-NA, November 1982. The model estimates maximum growth rates in military production for specified growth rates in civil consumption, and vice versa, subject to certain constraints. Realizing the specified (or maximized) consumption growth rates requires optimal allocation of output for civil investment as well as for end-use civil consumption. Hence, consumption growth covers *total* civil production, i.e., investment goods, as well as consumption goods.

Table 11

EFFECTS OF ALTERNATIVE COSTS OF EMPIRE ON GROWTH OF SOVIET CIVIL CONSUMPTION AND MILITARY PRODUCTION, 1980–1990
(In percent)

	Annual Growth of Civil Consumption as a Function of Annual Growth of Military Production (AGMP)					
AGMP =	0.0	2.0	4.5	7.0	9.0	10.5
Costs of the Soviet Empire (CSE) as a Percent of Soviet GNP, 1980-1990:						
1.6 (base case)	3.62	3.26	2.67	1.84	.94	.03
3.0 (1980 dollar CSE)	3.39	3.00	2.37	1.53	.60	-.32
4.0 (1970s ruble CSE)	3.19	2.78	2.12	1.25	.30	-.66
7.0 (1980 ruble CSE)	2.66	2.24	1.54	.58	-.51	-1.62

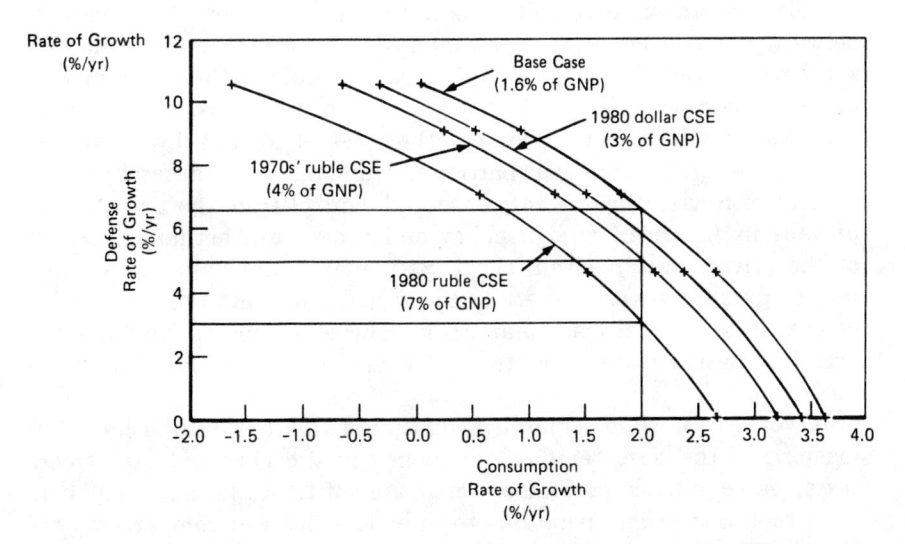

Fig. 4—Effects of alternative costs of empire on growth of Soviet civil consumption and military production, 1980–1990

percent in the intervening decade, and only 63 percent above the 1980 level if the annual miitary growth rate were 5 percent.

Compared with the base case of 1.6 percent of GNP, a 7 percent ratio of CSE to Soviet GNP would have the effect of reducing possible military production growth from an annual rate of 5 percent to less than 3 percent, assuming that civil consumption were maintained at the 2 percent annual growth rate.

In general, if aggregate consumption growth is held at 2 or 3 percent per year, each increase of 1 percent in the CSE ratio to GNP reduces the attainable annual growth rate of military production by 0.6 to 1 percent for each year of the decade. Alternatively, if annual military production were to grow between 4 and 5 percent, each increase of 1 percent in the CSE ratio to GNP would reduce annual growth in civil consumption by about 0.3 percent.

We will consider later possible U.S. and Western policies that might contribute to raising CSE appreciably above their recent levels, thereby imposing further constraints on possible rates of growth in Soviet production capabilities.

THE COSTS OF THE SOVIET AND U.S. EMPIRES

Another basis for assessing the relative size of CSE is to compare them with the putatively comparable costs of the U.S. "empire" (CUSE).

This comparison shouldn't obscure the profound noncomparabilities between the two empires. For example, the nature of U.S. relationships within the NATO alliance is fundamentally different from that between the Soviet Union and the members of the Warsaw Pact. Outside the formal alliance structures, the roles of force, subversion, and the international communist parties are fundamentally different in the spheres of Soviet imperial influence and control from the pattern that prevails in American foreign policy endeavors. Furthermore, the role of the private sector within the U.S. economy and polity is a major noncomparability with respect to the formulation and implementation of U.S. international trade and credit policies, compared with the role exercised by the state in controlling such decisions in the Soviet system.

Nevertheless, while acknowledging these and other differences in the meaning of the term "empire" as applied in the U.S. and Soviet contexts, we have made preliminary estimates of the following component costs of U.S. foreign operations to provide a basis of comparison with the costs of the Soviet empire: U.S. economic aid expenditures;

military aid expenditures, both budget and "off-budget"; and Export-Import Bank loans. As in the case of our previous estimate of CSE, we exclude commercial arms exports, as well as all direct U.S. military costs, including those incurred for U.S. forces stationed in NATO, and U.S. overseas bases. We also exclude estimates of the costs of U.S. covert activities abroad. There is nothing comparable in the portfolio of U.S. overseas costs to the implicit trade subsidies incurred by the Soviet Union in its dealings with other CMEA members. The results of this comparison between CUSE and CSE are shown in Table 12.

As Table 12 shows, the costs of the Soviet empire are relatively much larger than the comparable costs of the U.S. empire. Over the 1971-1980 decade, CSE as a share of Soviet GNP averaged 1.6 percent in dollars and 3.5 percent in rubles, whereas CUSE represented an average share of U.S. GNP of only 0.37 percent. If CSE are adjusted by subtracting the estimated Soviet costs of covert and destabilization activities[3] relating to the empire, the CSE dollar ratio to Soviet GNP decreases to 1.2 percent, and the ruble CSE(R) ratio decreases to 3.1 percent, still three to eight times as large as the corresponding ratio of CUSE to U.S. GNP.

BENEFITS

From the standpoint of the Soviet leadership, the ultimate criterion for assessing the relative size of CSE is the benefits—especially political, military, and strategic benefits—ascribed to the empire's maintenance and expansion.

Although it is not the purpose of this study to examine in detail the various benefits that the Soviet leadership may ascribe to the empire, Fig. 5 lists some of these elements. (The reference in the chart to "perceived" benefits, with quotation marks framing the word "perceived," implies that what we are dealing with here is *our* perception of the leadership's perception; thus, perceptions twice removed!)

The Soviet leadership probably highly values the political and strategic benefits ascribed to the maintenance and expansion of the Soviet empire. The empire constitutes a source of prestige, political prominence, and Russian national pride, that gratify the Soviet leadership and perhaps important constituencies as well. Generally, the leadership may veiw the assets represented by the empire as constituting a considerable amount of strategic leverage for thwarting the countervailing influence and political prominence of the United States. In a

---

[3]The reason for this adjustment is that our estimates for CUSE do not include any corresponding costs for U.S. covert activities abroad.

Table 12

COSTS OF THE SOVIET EMPIRE COMPARED WITH COSTS OF THE U.S. EMPIRE, 1971–1980

(Billions of current dollars)

	1971	1972	1973	1974	1975	1976	1977	1978	1979	1980
1. U.S. Economic aid	2.8	3.1	2.1	2.9	3.6	5.0	3.9	4.6	4.7	5.6
2. U.S. Military aid (budgetary and nonbudgetary)	1.0	0.7	0.8	1.3	2.0	3.1	2.0	2.0	1.9	2.8
3. Export-Import Bank loans	0.2	0.2	0.6	1.2	1.5	0.9	0.3	-0.1	0.2	1.8
4. Total costs of the U.S. "empire" (CUSE)	4.0	4.0	3.5	5.4	7.1	9.0	6.2	6.5	6.8	10.2
5. Total CUSE in constant 1981 dollars	8.2	7.8	6.5	9.2	11.0	13.3	8.6	8.5	8.2	11.1
6. CUSE as share of U.S. GNP (%)[a]	.38	.34	.27	.38	.46	.52	.32	.31	.29	.39
7. CSE as dollar share of Soviet GNP (%)[b]	1.12	.95	1.28	1.78	1.40	1.59	1.61	1.49	2.16	2.67
8. CSE (a) ruble share of Soviet GNP (%)[c]	1.78	1.68	2.54	3.70	2.94	3.67	3.78	3.50	5.15	6.64
9. Adjusted CSE* as dollar share of Soviet GNP (%)[d]	.63	.48	.84	1.36	1.02	1.23	1.27	1.16	1.84	2.36
10. Adjusted CSE* as ruble share of Soviet GNP (%)[e]	1.39	1.28	2.14	3.32	2.54	3.27	3.40	3.12	4.76	6.24

* CSE figures adjusted by removing costs of covert operations and destabilization activities (Row 6 in Table 1 and Table 4).

SOURCES: Budget of the U.S. Government, 1970–1983; Table 1 above. The implicit U.S. GNP deflator was used to convert current to constant 1981 dollars.

[a] 1971-80 average: 0.37 percent
[b] 1971-80 average: 1.6 percent
[c] 1971-80 average: 3.5 percent
[d] 1971-80 average: 1.2 percent
[e] 1971-80 average: 3.1 percent

1. *Political Benefits*
   - influence, power, international prestige, national pride
   - system justification, and consolidation at home
2. *Military Benefits*
   - force "multipliers" (bases, time-on-station, sortie generation, readiness, intelligence)
   - proxy forces (development and logistic support)

Fig. 5—Benefits derived or "perceived" from the Soviet empire

larger and perhaps more important sense, the empire may provide a source of legitimacy and justification for the sacrifices and deprivation that the Soviet system imposes on its citizens. Recalling our earlier citation from Milovan Djilas, there may be, or may be believed to be, a direct relationship between efforts by the leadership "to avoid internal problems" and to "go for expansion" of the Soviet empire. To this extent, the empire's importance to the leadership may be hard to exaggerate.

There are also certain tangible military benefits, such as bases and other facilities in Cuba and in Viet Nam, that contribute measurably and substantially to increasing the effectiveness and time-on-station of Soviet naval and other forces. In this sense, the empire acts to multiply the effectiveness of Soviet forces. Alternatively, such facilities can be thought of as saving the costs the Soviets would otherwise have to incur to achieve the same force effectiveness in the absence of these facilities. Such bases can also provide staging and recovery areas for use by Soviet ground and air forces, and can increase access to or control of supplies of critical materials, such as oil from the Persian Gulf. Some of the Soviet Union's imperial activities clearly have these effects—for example, the presence of Soviet forces in Afghanisvan within direct operational distance of the Straits of Hormuz, Soviet presence in Ethiopia in relation to control of the Horn of Africa, and the growth of Soviet military presence in Syria.

In sum, maintenance and expansion of the empire provides large strategic advantages to the Soviet Union in its competition with the United States. Although these political, military, and strategic benefits of the empire are noteworthy, certain noneconomic costs also accompany the empire's expansion. For example, Soviet support for Vietnam is one of the principal causes of the worsened relations between the

Soviet Union and China, and Soviet occupation of Afghanistan has impaired Soviet relations with parts of the Third World as well as with China.

Nevertheless, it is probably a reasonable presumption that the total costs—both noneconomic and economic—of the Soviet empire, at the levels they have reached in recent years, are likely to appear to the Soviet leadership to be quite reasonable, if not modest, in relation to this formidable package of benefits ascribed to the empire. Finally, our dollar estimates of CSE seem to be well within the bounds that have been acceptable to imperial powers in the past, whereas the ruble estimates toward the end of the 1970s had reached levels that seemed to be transcending those bounds.

VI. PROSPECTIVE COSTS AND IMPLICATIONS FOR U.S. POLICY

What are likely to be the costs of empire incurred by the Soviet Union during the 1980s? How should U.S. policy respond to the Soviet empire and its associated costs? Although this study does not provide answers to either of these questions, it does suggest some considerations that will affect the answers.

First, consider the question of prospective CSE in the 1980s. It is useful to distinguish between two aspects of these costs:

1. The costs of maintaining and expanding the empire (which we will refer to as M&E). Maintenance and expansion costs represent production costs—the economic costs of "producing" the empire in the sense of sustaining or expanding it;
2. The willingness of Soviet leadership to incur these costs. "Willingness" represents the inclination or preference on the part of the Soviet leadership to maintain and expand the empire in comparison with other objectives.

If we had a fully developed theory of the determinants of the Soviet empire, we might be able to formulate a cost model including botL production (M&E) aspects of costs and willingness (W) aspects. The dependent variable of the model would be the expected costs of the Soviet empire in time period t, which could be estimated as a function of the costs of production (the M&E aspects), and the demand (W aspects) of the empire in the same or a lagged time period. Our study does not provide such a model, but it suggests several factors that will raise or lower CSE during the 1980s.

Among the factors influencing M&E costs, some are likely to reduce and others to raise these costs in the 1980s compared with their levels toward the end of the preceding decade. The principal factors tending to reduce both total and marginal M&E costs are the following:

1. At least in the early part of the 1980s, the large fraction of total CSE that has been in the form of trade subsidies is likely to be reduced by the automatic workings of the pricing formula the Soviets use in their trade with other CMEA countries. Since 1977, the prices of these transactions have been based on five-year moving averages of world market prices for the commodities involved in this trade. During this time, and

particularly in 1978 and 1979, prices of Soviet exports, especially crude oil and oil products, have risen much more sharply in world markets than have prices of the manufactured goods that the Soviet Union imports from Eastern Europe. As a result, implicit trade subsidies escalated dramatically. This accounts for the sharp increase in the trade subsidies' component of total CSE at that time. At least for the first half of the 1980s, prices of oil, oil products, and other raw materials exported by the Soviet Union to its trading partners are likely to be much more stable. Hence, the five-year moving average price formula will result in transaction values much closer to current world market prices than was the case in the 1970s, thereby lowering the export component of implicit trade subsidies.

2. The Soviet Union has in recent years, started to ask or demand partial payment by client states for the military and technical services provided by Soviet forces and technicians. In some cases, such as Afghanistan, the Soviets are evidently trying to offset parts of their M&E costs by shipments of natural gas and other products from Afghanistan to reduce Afghanistan's "debt" to the Soviet Union.[1]

By contrast, several other factors will tend to raise M&E costs:

1. As noted in the previous discussion of historical cost patterns of other empires, M&E costs tend to rise as the social, cultural, and ethnic stresses and strains develop from the uncomfortable and sometimes hostile relationships between the superior, subsidizing, or "hegemonic" metropolitan country and its satellite. In the Soviet empire, these strains have obviously been most intense in Afghanistan and show indications of increasing still further. One symptom is the heightened scale of Afghan resistance to the Soviet occupation, and the higher annual costs borne by the Soviets compared with our estimates for 1980. Indications of strains in the Soviet Union's relationship to Ethiopia and North Korea may also entail or portend higher Soviet costs.

2. The increasingly serious economic predicament of the Eastern European members of CMEA, most notably Poland and Rumania, is likely to impose additional burdens of support on the Soviet Union, especially if this predicament cannot be relieved by their drawing on additional credits from the West.

---

[1] See the article on "Russia and the Afghan Economy" in *The Wall Street Journal*, September 16, 1981.

3. If the United States and its allies are able to work out a more concerted policy for reducing the subsidization of trade transactions with Eastern Europe than those that have undergirded these transactions in the 1970s, the result will also tend to increase CSE in the 1980s.

Similarly, some factors will tend to increase Soviet willingness to incur the costs of empire, and others are likely to reduce that willingness.

1. Expansion of Soviet influence and presence abroad is likely to be high among the values and objectives maintained by the Soviet leadership. Not only is the empire valued in itself, but it also provides a justification for maintaining economic and political restrictions at home. Notwithstanding increased CSE toward the end of the 1980s, expansion of the empire in the 1970s may have been plausibly viewed by the Soviet leadership as entailing an attractive ratio between incremental benefits and incremental costs. If, therefore, the empire appears to be a "good deal" to Soviet leaders, they will probably be willing to incur additional costs as long as this ratio remains, at the margin, what it has been during the past decade. Moreover, the Soviet leadership may even view the existing ratio of benefits to costs as one that involves political-economic "rents" for the Soviet Union: that is, a considerable margin of net benefits above costs. If this is so, leadership would be willing to incur increases in CSE even if the ratio of costs to benefits were to rise somewhat above what it has been in the past decade.
2. On the other hand, the Soviet economy is currently encountering serious difficulties in terms of declining rates of growth, rising capital-output ratios, declining productivity of both labor and capital inputs, and diminution in apparent worker incentives for high productivity because of consumption constraints. Thus, the competing claims of both the domestic economy, and the high rate of Soviet military spending in the 1980s, will tend to decrease, or at least constrain, the willingness of the leadership to incur further CSE.

We are in no position to judge what will be the balance between factors tending to raise and those tending to lower the costs of empire in the 1980s. However, we should consider whether there are ways by which U.S. policy might affect the balance, and whether the United States should attempt to do so.

Are there means by which the U.S. might seek to raise the costs of empire to the Soviet Union, and thereby to discourage its further expansion? Are there other means by which centrifugal tendencies within the noncontiguous empire might be encouraged?

One obvious means of raising the costs to the Soviet Union of maintaining its empire is to deny, or restrict, credit extended to countries within the empire. As a result, economic burdens that have been, in effect, diverted to the West would adhere to the empire itself. The extent to which these burdens would in turn be imposed on the Soviet Union, thereby raising CSE in the 1980s, is admittedly uncertain, for it is hard to fathom what will influence opening of the Soviet "umbrella" to support its client states in Eastern Europe, Cuba, and elsewhere. However, external sources of credit do reduce the likelihood of resource strains upon the Soviet Union. Consequently, restricting such credit, and certainly removing the subsidies that have supported them during the 1970s, would tend to increase CSE in the next decade.[2]

Outside the contiguous parts of the Soviet empire, other objectives and policy measures are worth considering. These differing objectives include encouragement and support for the centrifugal tendencies within the empire, as well as raising the costs to the Soviet Union of maintaining or expanding its influence and control in these areas.

One reason why the costs of expanding the Soviet empire have been relatively modest in the 1970s is that U.S. policy has lacked any means of dealing with certain instruments the Soviets use in this process. An example is provided by the activities of allied Cuban, East German, and Vietnamese forces supplied, trained, and supported financially and otherwise by the Soviet Union. Effective use of this military instrument has been complemented by the Soviet doctrine of supporting wars of national liberation. In turn, these combined political and military instruments have permitted the Soviet empire to expand apace and at quite modest cost.

At present, the United States has limited means of countering the Soviet Union's use of such allied forces in the Third World. To reshape existing U.S. policy so that it deliberately seeks to reverse expansion of the empire, as well as to raise the total costs of maintaining the empire, may require a combination of new declaratory policies and other measures relating to the programming of U.S. military and economic assistance, and to the conduct of U.S. diplomacy. This is not the place to go into detail on such ideas, which have been dealt with more fully elsewhere.[3] One part of this proposal is for the United

---

[2]For an analysis of these subsidies, see Daniel F. Kohler and Kip T. Fisher, *Subsidization of East-West Trade Through Credit Insurance and Loan Guarantees,* The Rand Corporation, N-1951-USDP, November 1982.

[3]See Charles Wolf, "Beyond Containment, Redesigning American Policies," *Washington Quarterly,* Winter 1982. A more complete version of this paper was published in September 1982 by the California Seminar on International Security and Foreign Policy. See also Charles Wolf, "Extended Containment," in Aaron Wildavsky (ed.), *Beyond Containment,* Institute of Contemporary Studies, San Francisco, California, 1983.

States to join with countries in the Third World having converging interests in developing a collaborative group of "associated country forces." In circumstances of mutual interest and concern to the participants, such forces might provide an effective counter to communist proxy forces in Third World areas.[4] Another part of such a policy would provide increased support for indigenous forces, such as those represented by the Afghan resistance fighters seeking liberation from Soviet imperialism.[5]

Finally, more attention and more information concerning the costs of the Soviet empire could profitably be disseminated both within the alliance, and perhaps as well in the Soviet Union. Those members of the Soviet elites who believe that the empire is a good deal for the Soviet Union are probably already acquainted with the associated costs, but others who perhaps have reasons for skepticism about the empire may be unaware of the true magnitude of these costs. In particular, those elites concerned with improvement of the civil economy, and not fully informed about the magnitude of the drains placed on the Soviet economy by the demands of maintaining and expanding the empire, might find this information of interest. Within the Western Alliance itself, awareness of the total sum of Soviet imperial efforts and their associated costs is quite limited. Perhaps better information on the entire subject of the costs of the Soviet empire would be worthwhile to disseminate in the interests of encouring more informed discussion within the Western Alliance, in the Soviet Union itself, and in such other interested countries as China.

The estimates presented in this study have been based on a wide range of sources with differing degrees of reliability and inclusiveness. Consequently, further work on the following specific topics would be warranted to improve the coverage and reliability of our estimates, as well as to up-date them:

---

[4]See *Beyond Containment*, California Seminar on International Security and Foreign Policy, September 1982, p. 17 ff.

[5]Samuel Huntington has advanced a related set of proposals for reversing the spread of the Soviet empire by attempts to "wean" or to "weaken" particular client states. For some parts of the empire (e.g., Ethiopia, Angola, Yemen), he suggests "encouraging opposition groups, promoting and supporting insurrection," thereby contributing to the empire's contraction. This part of his proposal is similar to the suggestions made above. For other parts of the empire (e.g., Eastern Europe), he proposes instead Western efforts and offers to promote "economic, diplomatic, and cultural engagement with Western societies." This "weaning" strategy is intended to loosen the bonds of the Soviet empire and recalls some of the expectations often associated with detente. To the extent that such attempts led the Soviets to compete with these Western efforts, CSE might be increased. However, the result might instead simply be to relieve the Soviet Union of a part of the burdens of support it would otherwise bear, thereby lowering CSE. See Samuel P. Huntington (Ed.), *The Strategic Imperative*, Chapter I, "The Renewal of Strategy," Ballinger, Cambridge, MA 1982.

1. Incremental costs of Cuban, East German, and Nicaraguan allied or proxy forces that are not already included in economic or military aid or any of the other cost categories included in our estimates. Such estimates might be arrived at by comparing data on the equipment and operating modes of these proxy forces with the specific types of military equipment and replacement parts already included in Soviet military deliveries to Cuba, East Germany and Nicaragua. Significant discrepancies between the two lists would suggest categories of incremental costs for these proxy forces that should be added to our previous estimates.

2. Incremental costs connected with the stationing of 32 Soviet divisions in Eastern Europe and with the construction and operation of Soviet bases in Cuba, Viet Nam, and elsewhere. To the extent that these external costs exceed the costs of the same Soviet forces based within the geographic limits of the Soviet Union itself, they might legitimately be ascribed to the costs of empire.

3. Allowance for economic offsets to CSE. The Soviets may obtain several types of offsets for the costs we have ascribed to the empire: for example, debt instruments in return for some military and economic aid, hard-currency payments to Soviet technicians in foreign countries, labor imported from parts of the empire into the Soviet Union and paid at wages below its marginal productivity. Although we believe these offsets are likely to be fairly small in the aggregate, a complete costing of the Soviet empire should should allow for such offsets, which we have not been able to do in this study.

4. Finally, up-dating the estimates to cover 1981–1983. Fragmentary data for most of the cost elements covered in CSE are available through 1981, and perhaps later. There have been recent changes in the international oil market and their effect on the export pricing formula used by the Soviet Union in its transactions with CMEA countries, so more recent data might show considerable changes in the export component of implicit trade subsidies entering into CSE. Consequently, it would be useful to try to update our estimates as close to the present as possible. More generally, it would be worthwhile to set up an information tracking mechanism within the government to monitor CSE on a regular and current basis.

Appendix

PRELIMINARY ESTIMATES OF COSTS INCURRED BY THE SOVIET UNION FOR COVERT OPERATIONS AND RELATED ACTIVITIES IN THE SOVIET EMPIRE

by Edmund Brunner, Jr.

INTRODUCTION

This appendix summarizes an exploratory effort to analyze the costs to the USSR of conducting covert and related destabilization and other activities throughout its empire, to note the relevant data sources available at Rand, and to arrive at preliminary estimates of these costs. The conceptual and data problems confronting this effort are formidable and will be addressed below. The estimates presented here have been developed entirely from open sources. They should be thought of as a preliminary, order-of-magnitude exercise intended to elicit comments and suggestions that might contribute to making better estimates in the future.

METHODOLOGY AND DATA

Normal cost analysis procedures are exacting, detailed, and definitionally and mathematically precise; nonetheless, they often yield highly inaccurate results. In the present case, available information does not allow us to pursue normal procedures. However, using the shaky evidence available and eclectic methods, we present preliminary estimates of the total cost of Soviet covert and agitprop operations related to the maintenance and expansion of the Soviet empire.

For covert (including security) operations, the method consists of making estimates of numbers of personnel engaged in intelligence, counterintelligence, subversion, terrorism, internal security, and support of fronts and communist parties in foreign countries. We then apply to these numbers a cost factor that includes investment and operating outlays. The personnel estimates were arrived at by: (a) adopting those published by the International Institute for Strategic Studies (IISS), the Annual Report of the Secretary of Defense, the Narkhoz,[1] etc.; (b) applying judgment to the evidence supplied by Barron, Penkovskiy, and other unofficial sources; and (c) reasoning by analogy from U.S. experience. For propaganda operations conducted by radio and television broadcasting and the production and distribution of publications (newspapers, periodicals, books), we arrived at our estimates by crude analogy, using US/SU ratios of newspaper circulation, numbers of books published, number of radio and TV stations, and U.S. figures on receipts by each industry.

A single cost per person was derived from CIA's "Estimated Soviet Defense Spending: Trends and Prospects," SR 78-10121, June 1978. Total defense spending in 1977 was estimated at between 53 and 58 billion rubles; we use their average, 55.5 billion. Using CIA's figures for military manpower in the five Soviet services and making an 8 percent allowance for overhead functions yields a total manpower estimate of 3.81 million in the Soviet military. Dividing the two figures results in a per person cost of about 14,570 rubles. Because we are using total military spending in the numerator, this figure includes investment as well as consumable manpower support.

COST ESTIMATION

Personnel

The USSR is run by a dual bureaucracy, governmental and party. The party is essentially the checker, the enforcer; its personnel are at every level and office of the governmental and military structures. We assume all party officials are part (overt) of the covert and related apparatus. In the government bureaucracy at all levels there were in 1980 2,495,000 administrative employees working in "general administrative bodies, the judiciary, police and fire protection, agricultural services, and various municipal services such as garbage collection, and street maintenance."[2] How many are concerned with "normal" law and order, and how many with more sinister activities?

A minimal estimate of the "normal" component might, with reservations and uncertainty, be drawn from a few analogies with U.S.

---

[1]Narodnoye Khozyaystvo SSSR, 1980.

[2]Joint Economic Committee, "Soviet Economy in a Time of Change," U.S. Congress, 1981 Session. The reference appears in a paper by Imogene Edwards, Margaret Hughes, and James Noren, "U.S. and USSR: Comparisons of GNP," Vol. I, p. 387.

experience. In 1979 there were 15,971,000 U.S. federal, state, and local employees, of whom 1,178,000, or 4–1/2 percent, were in the police, the judiciary, legal services, public defense and corrections. (*Statistical Abstract of the United States,* 1981.) Although these figures apparently include the FBI and DIA, they exclude the CIA and NSA. The FBI conducts covert as well as overt operations within the United States and the DIA, CIA, and NSA conduct covert operations in the Unite States. The Rockefeller Committee on Intelligence reported that the CIA conducted, over an unspecified time periods operations involving 300,000 individuals and organizations in the United States (*New York Times,* June 11, 1975). There seem to be several thousand security personnel in the federal government and many more in state and local police. As a very rough guess, drawing on these several indicators, we use a figure of 100,000 in the FBI, DIA, Army, Navy, Air Force, and state and local police, excluding CIA and NSA. Clearly, the Soviet "normal" contingent is much larger. As a preliminary figure, we attribute 200,000 to the "regular" Soviet governmental police organs within the USSR. Just as the U.S. *Statistical Abstract* data exclude CIA-NSA personnel, we assume that the Soviet Narkhoz excludes KGB/GRU/MVD personnel. Therefore, these will have to be added later.

All employees of the party can perhaps be regarded as required for maintenance of the Soviet system. Only one source[3] has been discovered so far that provides an estimate of the number of party *apparatchiki.* It estimates that in 1970 the party had about 200,000 full-time officials and employees. (A more accurate estimate would probably be closer to 500,000.) Between 1970 and 1980 the number of government administrative employees rose by 32–1/2 percent.[4] We assume a similar increase for the Party, thus yielding an estimate of 265,000 party bureaucrats helping or hindering those in the governmental apparatus. Assuming an average allocation of perhaps 30 to 35 employees from the party to each of 161 foreign countries, yields a total of, say, 5000 abroad and 260,000 at home.

We turn now to the KGB (Committee of State Security—Komitet Gosudarstvennoi Bezopasnosti), the principal secret intelligence, police, and clandestine service of the USSR. It has agents worldwide as well as an internal force of border guards numbering about 300,000. One can find an enormous range of estimates of the total number of KGB operatives, from 15,000 to 17,000,000. According to Victor Gouzenko, a

---

[3]John S. Reshetar, Jr., *The Soviet Polity,* Dodd Mead, New York and Toronto, 1972, p. 144.

[4]"Tsentral'noe statisticheskoe upravlenie SSSR," *Narodnoe Khoziaistvo SSSR v 1980g. statisticheskoe ezhegodhik,* "Finansy i statistika," Moscow, 1981.

defector from the Soviet Embassy in Ottawa, the USSR has "thousands, yes thousands of agents in the United States, thousands in Great Britain, and many other thousands spread elsewhere." Arkady Shevchenko, a high-ranking Soviet diplomat stationed at the United Nations in New York who defected in 1978, stated that the Soviet U.N. mission included about 300 KGB operatives. In 1971, Britain's Foreign Minister Sir Alec Douglas-Home complained in a letter to Gromyko of the hundreds of Soviet intelligence agents in Britain. A book written and published by *U.S. News and World Report* claimed that the KGB has 250,000 agents outside the USSR.[5] A more sober estimate is provided by John Barron of 90,000 agents worldwide.[6] Oleg Penkovskiy, who defected to the West in the early 1960s, revealed that the KGB and GRU (military intelligence) have agents in the diplomatic corps, the military, and in nearly all government organizations.[7] Penkovskiy stated in his book that in 1961 there was a total "of 3000 staff intelligence officers out of the 5200 Soviet representatives in the Soviet embassies and consulates in some 72 non-Communist countries." Furthermore, additional diplomatic personnel were believed to be coopted for intelligence work, leaving only 20 percent as "pure diplomats." In addition, there are many agents, "illegals and sleepers," not associated with the diplomatic service. Although the KGB clearly runs worldwide operations, Robert Conquest maintains "that the major part of the KGB's effort, the greater number of its employees, are used in the massive and continuous work against its own population."[8]

Starting with Barron's *circa* 1972 estimate of 90,000 operatives worldwide, and allowing for a 25 percent increase up to 1980 (paralleling the officially stated rise in the numbers of all governmental administrative employees), we arrive at a figure of 112,500. On the basis of Penkovskiy's and Conquest's statements, I guess that most of these are at home—97,500—and the remaining 15,000 are stationed in the 161 foreign countries around the world. The 300,000 KGB border guards generally have no function outside the USSR and are stationed wiihin its frontiers. Penkovskiy indicates that the GRU (military intelligence) is a rather small service; he was a member of it and should know. For the moment I'll ignore it, although the situation may have changed since Penkovskiy's era.

In addition to the border guards of the KGB, a separate organization, the Ministry of Internal Affairs (MVD) maintains internal

---

[5]*Famous Soviet Spies: The Kremlin's Secret Weapon*, U.S. News and World Report, Washington, D.C., 1973.

[6]John Barron, *KGB*, Bantam Books, New York 1974.

[7]Oleg Penkovskiy, *The Penkovskiy Papers*, Doubleday, New York, 1965.

[8]Barron, *KGB*.

security troops of about 150,000 men.[9] Like the KGB border guards, these troops normally have no function outside the USSR and are stationed within its frontiers to cope with internal security problems.[10] The Soviet Union supports external units besides the KGB. The USSR has many thousands of civilian and military advisers in foreign countries and also trains and supports terrorists in some of them. According to Secretary of Defense Weinberger, the Soviet Union maintains 45,680 civilian and military advisors in 19 foreign countrfes, not counting the 87,000 troops in Afghanistan.[11] If Shevchenko, Gouzenko, Penkovskiy, and others are correct, the advisors are engaged in the sorts of activities relevant to our costing exercise. They are therefore included in our estimate and their costs are identified separately.

The USSR trains and helps support an unknown number of people in terrorist organizations abroad. A perusal of numerous Rand studies in this field suggests that the actual numbers of terrorists are rather small, as is the cost of supporting them. For example, the German Red Army Faction (Baader-Meinhof) had about 70 "full-time" terrorists in 1980 and only about 12–15 by August 1981. German officials estimate the cost per person at about $50,000 annually.[12] The Red Brigade in Italy has perhaps 150 full-time members supported at an annual cost of about $15,000 each.[13] Colombia apparently has about 3000 terrorists receiving Soviet support.[14] Other terrorists (in Ulster and the Mideast) may also receive some help from the USSR.[15]

Based on these diverse, suggestive, but inconclusive indicators, we assume an *average* of 200 Soviet-supported terrorists in each of 115 non-Communist countries, for a total of 23,000.

Considering the German estimate of $50,000 per man and the Italian estimate of $15,000 per man, our earlier estimate of 14,570 rubles seems to be a reasonable cost factor, translating to about $30,000–36,000 per man at plausible ruble/dollar exchange rates.

Besides the foregoing, we must still consider the media organizations (radio, press, journals), support of foreign Communist parties and fronts, and clandestine radios. By crude, and surely arguable, analogy with the United States, the Soviet radio and TV broadcasting

---

[9]IISS, *The Military Balance, 1981–82*.

[10]In unusual circumstances, such as past crises in Eastern Europe and Afghanistan, some of these forces have been used outside the Soviet Union.

[11]Caspar W. Weinberger, *Annual Report to the Congress*, FY 1983.

[12]Unpublished Rand research by G. V. Bass.

[13]Unpublished Rand research by B. Jenkins and S. Moran.

[14]Unpublished Rand research by W. F. Sater.

[15]Unpublished Rand research by G. M. Petty, and by B. J. Cordes.

enterprise costs about $30 billion a year, and publishing around $35 billion a year. Certainly a substantial part of this is devoted to the propaganda demands of the state.[16] But not all. The media also deal with ordinary news of daily affairs, the weather, and other nonpolitical matters. Lacking a basis for an accurate ratio, we make a rough judgment that 60 percent of the bill is for propaganda and 40 percent for other items. This results in a media propaganda outlay of close to $39 billion. To estimate the portion that should be attributed to the costs of external media propaganda and supporting Communist parties and fronts abroad, we have drawn from unclassified CIA data.

The Total Bill

The foregoing discussion has summarized an admittedly arguable basis for estimating the costs of Soviet covert and related operations for the Soviet Union as a whole, within the USSR, and in the external empire. Nine categories of expenditures were established:

Government law and order
Communist Party
KGB—Agents
    Guards (border)
MVD internal security troops
Civilian and military advisers abroad
Terrorist organizations
Media organizations
Support of Communist parties, fronts, etc., abroad

For the first seven categories, we estimated costs by applying a cost per man factor to estimates of personnel for each organizational component, as a whole and separately, within the USSR and in the external empire. In estimating cost of propaganda conducted through the media, we followed a different method, using analogy with the United States, plus some CIA data on costs of media operations in foreign countries. With respect to Soviet support of Communist parties and fronts in foreign countries, CIA estimates were accepted.

All of this material, for 1980, is brought together in Table A.1. In general, we first derived ruble cost estimates and then converted to dollars using dollar-ruble ratios:

---

[16]See Barich A. Hazan, *Soviet Propaganda: A Case Study of the Middle East Conflict*, John Wiley & Sons, New York and Toronto, 1975.

Table A.1

ESTIMATED COSTS OF THE SOVIET EMPIRE, FOR COVERT AND RELATED OPERATIONS, 1980

(In billions of rubles or dollars)

Organization	Number of Personnel Total	Number of Personnel USSR Only	Number of Personnel External Empire	Estimated Ruble Costs Total	Estimated Ruble Costs USSR Only	Estimated Ruble Costs External Empire	$2.47 per Ruble Total	$2.47 per Ruble USSR Only	$2.47 per Ruble External Empire	$2.08 per Ruble Total	$2.08 per Ruble USSR Only	$2.08 per Ruble External Empire	$0.94 per Ruble Total	$0.94 per Ruble USSR Only	$0.94 per Ruble External Empire
Government law and order	200,000	200,000	0	2.91	2.91	0	7.19	7.19	0	6.05	6.05	0	2.74	2.74	0
Communist party	265,000	260,000	5,000	3.86	3.79	0.07	9.53	9.36	0.17	8.03	7.88	0.15	3.63	3.56	0.07
KGB - Agents	112,500	97,500	15,000	1.64	1.42	0.22	4.05	3.51	0.54	3.41	2.95	0.46	1.54	1.33	0.21
- Guards	300,000	300,000	0	4.37	4.37	0	10.79	10.79	0	9.09	9.09	0	4.11	4.11	0
MVD internal security	150,000	150,000	0	2.19	2.19	0	5.41	5.41	0	4.56	4.56	0	2.06	2.06	0
Civilian and military advisers	45,680	0	45,680	0.67	0	0.67	1.65	0	1.65	1.39	0	1.39	0.63	0	0.63
Terrorist organizations	23,000	0	23,000	0.34	0	0.34	0.84	0	0.84	0.71	0	0.71	0.32	0	0.32
Media organizations	na	na	na	15.79	14.74	1.05[a]	39.00	36.41	2.59[a]	32.85	30.66	2.19[a]	14.84	13.85	0.99[a]
Communist parties, fronts, etc. abroad	na	na	na	0.15	0	0.15[a]	0.36	0	0.36[a]	0.31	0	0.31[a]	0.14	0	0.14[a]
TOTAL	--	--	--	31.92	29.42	2.50	78.82	72.67	6.15	66.40	61.19	5.21	30.01	27.65	2.36

[a] Based on unclassified CIA estimates appearing in "Soviet Covert Action (The Forgery Offensive)," Hearings before the Subcommittee on Oversight of the Permanent Select Committee on Intelligence, House of Representatives, 96th Congr., 2nd Sess., February 1980. In this volume the CIA estimates the total costs of covert and agitprop operations in the Soviet external empire *only* at $3.36 billion. They do not explain how they derive their estimates.

1. The 1977 GNP Soviet-weighted dollar-ruble ratio of 2.47/1 derived by Edwards, Hughes, and Noren.[17]
2. The 1977 defense-space Soviet-weighted dollar-ruble ratio of 2.08/1 derived by the same author.
3. The 1977 Soviet foreign trade turnover based dollar-ruble ratio of 0.94/1 derived by Treml and Kostinsky.[18]

The results in dollars are shown in the table. In the case of the CIA data on Soviet media and party/front support abroad, dollar estimates were converted to rubles using the GNP 2.47/1 ratio and then expressed in dollars using the alternate ratios.

Covert and related activities apparently cost the Soviet Union about 32 billion rubles a year, of which 30 billion rubles are assignable to the USSR at home and 2.5 billion to the external empire. Depending upon the dollar-ruble ratio used, these amounts translate into a bill ranging from $2.4 billion to $6.4 billion a year for the external empire.

Time Trends, 1971-1980

To obtain a rough impression of the trend of Soviet costs for covert and related activities, we estimated these corresponding costs for 1970. The results appear in Table A.2. Personnel numbers were adjusted downward for the following reasons, and then multiplied by the 14,570 ruble per man figure to obtain 1970 cost estimates:

1. Government law and order personnel — Adjusted by percentage change in budget for Government Administration (Narkhoz 1980, (1970 h 71 percent of 1980)

2. Communist Party personnel — Adjusted by the change in the number of Primary Party Organizations (1970 = 89.8 percent of 1980)

---

[17]*Soviet Economy in a Time of Change*, A Compendium of Papers Submitted to the Joint Economic Committee, Congress of the United States, 96th Cong., 1st Sess., Vol. I, Imogene Edwards, Margaret Hughes, and James Noren, "U.S. and USSR: Comparisons of of GNP."

[18]V. G. Treml and B. L. Kostinsky, *The Domestic Value of Soviet Foreign Trade: Exports and Imports in the 1972 Input-Output Table*, Bureau of the Census, October 1982, p. 16.

Table A.2

COMPARISON OF ESTIMATED COSTS OF SOVIET COVERT AND RELATED OPERATIONS, 1970 AND 1980

Organization	1970 Total	1970 USSR Only	1970 External	1980 Total	1980 USSR Only	1980 External	% Change 1970-1980 Total	% Change 1970-1980 USSR Only	% Change 1970-1980 External
Government law and order	2.07	2.07	0	2.91	2.91	0	40.6	40.6	(b)
Communist Party	3.47	3.40	0.07	3.86	3.79	0.07	11.2	11.5	(a)
KGB - Agents	1.24	1.07	0.17	1.64	1.42	0.22	32.3	32.7	29.4
- Guards	2.40	2.40	0	4.37	4.37	0	82.1	82.1	(b)
MVD internal security	1.24	1.24	0	2.19	2.19	0	76.6	76.6	(b)
Civilian and military advisers	0.09	0.0	0.09	0.67	0	0.67	644.4	(b)	644.4
Terrorist organizations	0.25	0	0.25	0.34	0	0.34	36.0	(b)	36.0
Media organizations	12.63	11.79	0.84	15.79	14.74	1.05	25.0	25.0	25.0
CPs, fronts, etc. abroad	0.11	0	0.11	0.15	0	0.15	36.4	(b)	36.4
TOTAL	23.50	21.97	1.53	31.92	29.42	2.50	35.8	33.9	63.4

[a]Insignificant.
[b]Not applicable.

3. KGB agents — Adjusted by reference to Barron; 1970 = 76 percent of 1980

4. KGB guards and MVD Internal security troops and civilian and military advisers, number of personnel — Adjusted by IISS Military Balance 1969/70 figures, varying percentages

5. Terrorist organization — Adjusted to conform to change in KGB estimate

6. Media costs — Adjusted by examination of changes in book, newspaper, and journal circulation, numbers of TV stations, ruble value of communications services 1970–1980 as shown in Narkhoz 1980

7. Costs of Communist parties, fronts, etc. — Same as KGB

Table A.2 shows estimated 1970 and 1980 costs in billions of current rubles and the percentage changes between the two dates. The average growth over the decade has been slightly over 5 percent annually. This annual growth rate was used to obtain the cost estimates for covert and related activities for the intervening years, 1971–1979. Of the total costs of Soviet covert and related activities in 1970, 6.5 percent were associated with the external empire; the corresponding share rose to 7.8 percent by 1980.